Prelude to Music Education

Joanne H. Erwin
Oberlin Conservatory of Music

Kay L. Edwards
Miami University of Ohio

Jody L. Kerchner
Oberlin Conservatory of Music

John W. Knight
Oberlin Conservatory of Music

pg. 73
#2, 3, 4
→ combine all 3
into a short
essay

Prentice Hall

Upper Saddle River, NJ 07458

Library of Congress Catalog-in-Publication Data

Prelude to music education / Joanne H. Erwin . . . [et al.].
   p. cm.
  Includes bibliographical references and index.
  ISBN 0-13-030414-X
   1. Music—Instruction and study. I. Erwin, Joanne H.

MT1.P715 2003
780'.71—dc21   2002025241

VP, Editorial Director: Charlyce Jones Owen
Senior acquisitions editor: Christopher T. Johnson
Production editor: Laura A. Lawrie
Manufacturing and prepress buyer: Benjamin D. Smith
Copy editor: Laura A. Lawrie
Editorial assistant: Evette Dickerson
Marketing manager: Christopher Ruel
Marketing assistant: Scott Rich
Director of Marketing: Beth Mejia
Cover design: Kathi L. Mello
Photographer: Al Fuchs

This book was set in 10.5/12 Palatino by TSI Graphics, Inc.

© 2003 by Pearson Education, Inc.
Upper Saddle River, New Jersey 07458

Printed in the United States of America

10 9 8 7 6 5 4

ISBN 0-13-030414-X

PEARSON EDUCATION LTD., London
PEARSON EDUCATION AUSTRALIA PTY, Limited, Sydney
PEARSON EDUCATION SINGAPORE, Pte. Ltd
PEARSON EDUCATION NORTH ASIA LTD, Hong Kong
PEARSON EDUCATION CANADA, LTD., Toronto
PEARSON EDUCACIÓN DE MEXICO, S.A. de C.V.
PEARSON EDUCATION--Japan, Tokyo
PEARSON EDUCATION MALAYSIA, Pte. Ltd
PEARSON EDUCATION, Upper Saddle River, New Jersey

Contents

Foreword

The Introduction to Music Education course has become such a staple in music teacher preparation programs that it is difficult to remember when the undergraduate major did not include this one. There *was* such a time, but we hardly can think of revisiting it.

The reason for the course's popularity is its essential function as a springboard for the rest of the study leading up to student teaching—that capstone of all capstone experiences. The reasons for the course's essential nature are the very needs that inspired its development in the first place: First, students preparing to be music teachers often had little knowledge of the field they were entering, except as it was revealed in their own musical backgrounds. If they were instrumentalists, they might be only peripherally aware of choral programs and even less so of general music instruction. Singers might not know anything about early string instruction; perhaps no one had experience with multicultural music education. And so forth. Requiring students to dive into content-intensive foundations and methods courses without a more general overview was rather like asking them to take a bite of something without being able to see what they were about to eat.

Second, students' time frame also was limited to their own experience, probably no more than fourteen years at most. The fact that they were about to join the ranks of passionate "school-music" professionals working since 1838 and might acquire an understanding of how school music teaching began and the ways it has changed and expanded seemed too important to ignore. Ours is a rich, colorful, and significant tradition; not to be informed by it in our present and future work would seem to short-change both.

Finally, but not least important, was the recognition that not all students enrolling in a music education major knew their calling. While some may have determined their life's work at a beginning piano lesson, more had come to a perhaps uncertain decision fairly recently, and still others were not at all sure that they could or wanted to teach music to school-aged learners. There needed to be an opportunity for students to dip their pre-professional toes into the music education waters and either confirm their resolve or resolve to do something else!

And so, the "intro course" was born and now is a standard feature of most music teacher education programs. What is *not* standard is the precise content, the number and nature of field experiences ("out there" in schools), or the ways in which it is taught. However, the four authors of the text you are beginning to read have team taught the introductory course for years, revising and honing along the way. They have managed to provide students with just the right balance of learning about music teaching, watching it happen, and beginning to practice the art. This is not to say that the course is always the same: Gifted, seasoned teachers always are instructed by their students, in much the same way that you will inform those teaching you. Thankfully, these four gifted, seasoned teachers have undertaken to ease your way into the tradition by collecting some of their wisdom between the covers of this text. Welcome!

Catherine Jarjisian, Director
Baldwin-Wallace College Conservatory of Music

Introduction

In the new millennium, we find the field of music education thriving and in need of more energetic, dedicated teachers. The Music Education Division at the Oberlin College Conservatory of Music in Ohio consists of four faculty specializing in elementary/multicultuarl music, secondary/choral music, orchestra and band. We have team-taught a first-year course—Introduction to Music Education—for several years and knew there was a need for a text that would be inviting, informative, and practical to students either already committed to or considering entering the music education profession.

Our Introduction to Music Education course is offered the first semester of our students' first year. Throughout the semester, we share our integrated approach toward music making, music research, and music teaching. In order to set the tone for each topic, each chapter opens with a scenario derived from our collective fifty-plus years of experience in public school music programs. Each chapter includes a lesson plan, discussion questions, and resources should students wish to pursue the topic further. Not only do each of the four authors have different career specializations, but also we have somewhat different writing styles. We have purposely opted to preserve that distinctiveness.

Prelude to Music Education represents our desire to help students develop a passion for sharing music with others and to help them peek through the porthole to see vast possibilities that a degree in music education opens to its graduates.

One other ingredient of each class we teach is the application of the *National Standards for Arts Education* as adopted by Music Educators National Conference: National Association of Music Education in 1992 and published in 1994. We choose to continue to refer to the organization as MENC.

Music Education Content Standards

1. Singing, alone and with other, a varied repertoire of music.
2. Performing on instruments, alone and with others, a varied repertoire of music.
3. Improvising melodies, variations and accompaniments.
4. Composing and arranging music within specified guidelines.
5. Reading and notating music.
6. Listening to, analyzing, and describing music.
7. Evaluating music and music performances.
8. Understanding relationships between music, the other arts, and disciplines outside the arts.
9. Understanding music in relation to history and culture.

ACKNOWLEDGMENTS

The music education faculty of Oberlin deeply appreciates the work Bree Banks and Jeanne Bay have done in assisting the editing and preparing of the text. Their cheerful and able work is invaluable. We also wish to thank the students and faculty of Oberlin Conservatory for enabling our teaching to be such a joy. In addition, we thank the following reviewers: Dr. Jeffrey E. Bush—Arizona State University; Dr. Pam Stover—Clarion University of Pennsylvania; Dr. Margaret Kelly—Illinois State University; and Dr. George Weimer—University of Indianapolis.

1

Becoming a Music Teacher

Two music students, Sam, an oboist, and Mark, a trombonist, are listening to Professor Adams, Chairman of the Music Education Division, explain the many opportunities in music teaching. Sam is excited about being an instrumental teacher and is very animated as he tells Professor Adams about the wonderful high school he attended with six full time music teachers who were a major influence on his life. It is because of their influence that he would like to dedicate his life to the field of music education. As Sam tells Professor Adams about their three-hundred-piece marching band that won the state championship and their wonderful wind ensemble that took Lincolnshire Posy to contest and received a I division rating, Mark sits uncomfortably in his seat reflecting about his own high school experience.

Mark came from an inner-city school that did not have a marching band but only a forty-piece concert band with one director who seemed to be overworked, burned out, and completely disenchanted with teaching. For the most part, Mark's experiences in high school band were extremely negative. However, the one positive thing that kept Mark in music was his trombone lessons with Mr. Jones, an outstanding teacher who taught at the local music store. It was through the influence of Mr. Jones that Mark decided to major in music performance in college.

Mark was brought out of this reverie when Professor Adams informed Sam that a large marching band is great but should be only one part of a balanced program that must be comprehensive for all students. To find out more about how to build a successful program that will fit the needs of all students, Professor Adams invited Sam and Mark to take Music Education 101. The topic for the first class will be "Becoming an Effective Music Teacher."

Perhaps you are sitting in this class trying to decide whether you should be a music teacher or a performer. This question need not worry you at this time, because it is possible to be both a teacher and a performer. In fact, the authors of this text are good examples of balancing teaching careers with that of being successful performers. The authors firmly believe that you cannot be a good music teacher unless you are also a good performer. You see, it is not a question of being a teacher or a performer, because great teaching is a performing art and a great performer is always teaching.

In order for you to focus on the relationship between teaching and performing, we would like for you to read the following quotes from an article entitled "Is Teaching a Performing Art?" (Woolum, 1980). Indicate if you agree (A) or disagree (D) and also consider how these quotes apply to music teaching in a classroom and/or rehearsal.

_____ 1. "Teaching involves interpreting, translating, and communicating. All communication has an element of performance in it."

_____ 2. "I don't see myself as a performer if performance is defined as delivery at the expense of content. But if performance is a process that extends from content, then I have been a performer for the past ten years."

_____ 3. "We start to believe that what we're teaching is intrinsically interesting, even when we are teaching students who don't know anything about the subject. That's where performance comes in. Teachers need to communicate their excitement—the drama of the subject."

_____ 4. "A teacher can't act. Students can tell that what he's saying doesn't ring true if he's pretending to be excited. Students are very tolerant, but they won't take sham."

_____ 5. "I am a performer in the sense that I want to have attention focused on me. Particularly in a very large class it's no small task to hold attention for fifty minutes. It's this ability that I equate with performance."

_____ 6. "I don't agree that a teacher should perform. I don't think a teacher should feel obligated to capture and keep student attention."

_____ 7. "I think the conveying of any intense experience or engagement with a subject matter has an element of drama in it. Teaching is a kind of risky drama. You're always playing yourself. You're not saying lines written by someone else, and your audience isn't there to fill leisure time."

Now that you are thinking about the interrelationship between teaching and performing, it is time to reflect on the reasons for choosing to be a music teacher. Many of us chose this profession because of the great influence certain teachers had on our musical growth in the past. Another reason may be that we simply love music and want to share that love with our students. Perhaps some of us would like to make a positive difference in the lives of young people through the power of music. Whatever the reason, this book will help you formulate your philosophy and experience a growing commitment to music education.

Sometimes the art of music teaching seems wrapped in an aura of mystery. When we look at the qualities of the great teachers that we have had in the past, however, certain common characteristics seem to emerge. Here is a summary and compilation of traits that describe an "effective teacher" in the opinion of past students.

An effective teacher:
- takes an interest in them; serves as an advisor; cares
- commands the respect of students in knowledge, ability, and discipline
- is open to suggestions; encourages students' exploration and discovery
- communicates well; can explain things in more than one way
- is enthusiastic about his/her teaching
- has a sense of humor and knows when to use it
- is willing to give extra help; takes time to meet individual needs
- has high standards about students' work; is particular and demanding
- has imaginative teaching approaches
- is encouraging; recognizes potential in students
- is patient
- is well organized
- has respect for others
- is inspiring
- is honest; recognizes his/her limitations

- is broadly educated; has many interests
- is diplomatic and tactful
- works well with all types of persons and can vary teaching approaches accordingly
- is fair; is flexible
- is dedicated; has a real desire to teach
- gives a personal touch; relates personal experiences
- stimulates students' imaginations
- sets a good example
- performs well
- does not have an overinflated ego
- is adaptable; can handle crises

The art of teaching has inspired some of our greatest minds to write about this fascinating subject. Consider the words of Kahlil Gibran from *The Prophet*: "If he is indeed wise he does not bid you to enter the house of his wisdom, but rather leads you to the threshold of your own mind" (Gibran, 1964). These words serve as a daily reminder that the teachers who have influenced us also were often great human beings. Perhaps the poet William Wordsworth put it best when he wrote, "The child is the father of the man" (1950, p. 308).

As musicians, the depth of our interpretations stems from our life experiences and the people who influenced us. For this reason, it is important to know more than just music.

The great conductor Bruno Walter once stated that "a musician who is only a musician is only half a musician" (1961, p. 106). By this, he meant that wisdom is gained by searching and reflecting within ourselves and within the minds of others. Great literature, art, and music not only increase our understanding of ourselves but also of humanity. If we are going to produce results in our students that are both technically acceptable and aesthetically meaningful, we as teachers must have broad artistic experiences. Viewed in this light, that we must go beyond the notes, teaching is a great art, and the profession of *music* teaching assumes a depth and breadth of exciting proportions.

To go beyond the notes means that we must teach substance over technique. Indeed, teaching is a performing art. Teaching music is more than having total mastery of your instrument, it goes much deeper than this. A poignant definition of a master teacher is given to us by the writer John Steinbeck (1958):

> School is not easy and it is not for the most part very much fun, but then if you are lucky, you may find a real teacher. Three real teachers in a lifetime is the very best of luck. I have come to believe that a great teacher is a great artist and there are as few as there are any great artist. Teaching might be the greatest of the arts since the medium is the human mind and the spirit.
>
> My three teachers had these things in common:
> 1. They all loved what they were doing.
> 2. They did not just tell us information, but they catalyzed a burning desire to know more.
> 3. Under their influence, the horizons sprang far and wide and fear of failing went away and the unknown became knowable.
> 4. But most important of all, the truth, that dangerous stuff, became very beautiful and very precious.

Steinbeck constantly reminds us that effective music teaching is more than a flashy technique or an ethereal philosophy; it should be and must be a performing art.

When the American composer George Crumb was asked to define music, he said, "Music might be defined as a system of proportions in the service of a spiritual impulse" (Gagne and Caras, 1982, p. 128). This definition means that each time we enter a classroom we should feel as though something wonderful and unique is going to happen. The more lasting and beautiful things in music and also in life cannot be seen; they must be felt. Unless we can inspire and teach the emotional significance of music, it means nothing. Our legacy is what we give to students; our reward is what students give us.

It is with this philosophy in mind that we have come to write *Prelude to Music Education*. The information in this book will guide you carefully and methodically through the creative steps that will transform music teaching into an art, and, in doing so, you will be changed from a passive recipient into an active participant in a wonderful profession.

ASSIGNMENT: MOST INFLUENTIAL TEACHER

Prepare a two-minute description and explanation of your most influential teacher, which will be presented in front of the class next week. This person does not have to be a music teacher or a public school teacher. You should give some thought to what characteristics were particularly memorable about this person. If you have trouble coming up with a person, think of the characteristics first and then perhaps a person will come to mind.

When you speak, pay attention to your posture, pace of speaking, enunciation, eye contact, and choice of words. This is a chance for your teachers and peers to not only to get to know you and what is important to you in a teacher, but to let you "break the ice" as a presenter. It is the first step in your teaching career!

REFERENCES

GAGNE, C. and CARAS, T. (1982). *Soundpieces: Interviews with American Composers*. Metuchen, NJ: Scarecrow Press.

GIBRAN, K. (1964). *The Prophet*. New York: Knopf.

STEINBECK, J. (1958). *On Teaching*. Retrieved July 2000 from <http://www.ousd.k12.ca.us/crl/iu/iu-bawp/steinbeckexcerpt.html>.

WALTER, B. (1961). *Of Music and Music Making*. New York: W.W. Norton.

WOOLUM, N. (1980). "Is Teaching a Performing Art?" *Old Oregon*, 60(2), pp. 8–11.

WORDSWORTH, W. (1950). "My Heart Leaps Up." *English Poetry and Prose of the Romantic Movement*. Chicago: Scott, Foresman.

2

Developing Tools
For Teaching

Over a break from my college, I decided to go back and visit my high school music teacher. When I entered the building, I was struck with the high energy of the students in the halls during class changes. The music room had a familiar look with chairs in the ready position, posters of musical motives and a banner proclaiming school pride. Ms. Liu was happy to see me and eager to hear about my new college life. I asked her about the choir and she described the differences from my years in the group, but that there was still a strong positive energy. I asked how she kept her passion going for teaching through the years and she said the students were the source of much of it. She also said that singing in her church choir did a lot to keep her own involvement alive.

The students came bounding in the room, so our conversation stopped as Ms. Liu directed her attention to them and to the start of rehearsal. She greeted students as they entered and the students checked the board for the day's agenda, got their music, and took a seat. Just after the start of class, Ms. Liu started with warmup stretches and vocalizing. I had remembered what a nice sense of settling into the group that these activities gave me. The exercises then were specifically related to the first piece of music and she launched into a very focused rehearsal. All the students were attentive and I was pleased to hear that the group sounded as good as I remembered from when I was in it. I was glad that I came and could see through different lenses the reasons why my high school musical experience did propel me on to study in this field.

This chapter will address several techniques teachers often use—observation, interviewing, maintaining a journal, and lesson planning—that are helpful to developing prospective music educators. In the early stages of teacher training, time spent actively observing and questioning other music educators in all types of musical settings and in a variety of school cultures is extremely beneficial. These types of activities help to develop a personal teaching style, classroom management strategies, and a "goodie bag" of teaching ideas that are creative and that overtly bring music to life in the classroom or ensemble setting.

OBSERVATION

In the dictionary, the definition of the word "observation" includes "the act, practice, or power of noticing, . . . and recording facts and events as for . . . study." It is noteworthy that the definition of "observation" implies active participation in that which is observed. Observation is not a passive act but, rather, an active engagement of all sensory modalities—hearing, seeing, feeling, smelling—so that the observer is able to gather information about a situation that is as holistic as possible.

Observation assists teachers in becoming better communicators and educators, because they have the opportunity to see, hear, and analyze words, phrases, and teaching techniques that work for other teachers. By contrast, observing that which is less effective in the classroom or in the rehearsal setting is also very useful information.

An important component of observation is the recording of sensory data in a nonjudgmental manner. This is a manner of assessing, not evaluating, the teaching. The role of the observer is to provide an objective record of that which she/he sees, hears, feels, experiences in a class. The onus, then, is on the observer to ask questions about the facts that were collected during the observation. Why did it appear that . . . ? Who/what influenced the teacher's decision to . . . ? What might have prompted the student's behavior . . . ? How did the teacher implement . . . ? What prior knowledge did the teacher possess that might have influenced that which I noticed in the rehearsal . . . ? What about the students' background might influence . . . ? What is affecting the classroom environment or atmosphere . . . ?

The observer's role is not to pass judgment on the teacher's techniques or on the teaching demonstration, because the observer notes only a slice of the entire classroom dynamics or of the ensemble program. It is the role of the observer to analyze and to speculate about various reasons for that which was observed. Until the observer compiles data of various sources and spends much time in the teaching environment, she/he is unable to draw any concrete conclusions. Observation for the understanding of a particular class or ensemble requires the observer to spend an extended period of time with that community.

Teachers observe not only students but also themselves and other teachers in order to refine their teaching skills and insights. Videotape provides an effective venue for self-evaluation. One of the interesting discoveries of people undertaking an observation study is that the subject of the observation does not have to be in our major area of expertise for the observer to gain knowledge and information. Peer observation—having colleagues observe and record what they see and hear during a particular class and then "debriefing" what the person observed—is also an effective tool for learning about others and self.

What to Observe?

So what exactly is there to observe? This is the first question to ask before entering the classroom or rehearsal setting. Here are some facets of instruction on which to focus your attention during an observation.

The physical setting of classrooms and rehearsal areas is one element to be observed, for it might greatly inform the teacher or preservice music educator about the experiences and musical opportunities that occur during the observation time. How desks are arranged, how chairs are placed, the availability of space for a band rehearsal or sectional rehearsal, the lighting, and the maintenance of the classroom or rehearsal setting may or may not be conducive for learning. Behavior and speech of students are also worthy of noting during an observation.

Often an observer captures a flavor of a classroom or rehearsal setting by including direct quotations from students' and teachers' verbal interactions. Many teachers spend a majority of the rehearsal talking! What do teachers say and how do teachers say it? Some researchers have found that the use of imagery and questioning increase the on-task participation of the students (Yarbrough, 1975). This would be a specific teaching technique to observe, for too much talking and not enough music-making is detrimental to the effectiveness of a class or rehearsal. Is there a balance? Why or why not?

The expressive dynamic of the teacher's voice also influences her/his effectiveness in teaching. Vocal expression and inflection are not merely what words are chosen but how the words are spoken. Variety is the "spice of life" and the element that keeps the spoken word interesting. If teachers speak in a monotone, students tend to become disinterested and disengaged. Studies have shown that the magnitude of delivery in the voice engages students' attention (Yarbrough, 1975).

Yet another facet important to understanding one's own teaching or someone else's teaching is nonverbal communication among students and between students and teachers. The body language displayed by students and/or teachers can clearly set the tone for a music class or rehearsal. It is surprising to realize that a major portion of our communication is done nonverbally and, even more explicitly, just with the face. When teachers view themselves on videotape, they know what they want to communicate, but they often are surprised to see delivery that might be unclear. How do teachers use their hands? Consider the gesture in response to a student's question, the preparatory gesture, the cue, or the cutoff. Is it helpful or confusing? Try teaching a class without talking to see how effective the nonverbal communication is.

Another observable aspect of teaching is the mobility of the teacher—her/his movement in the rehearsal space or in the music classroom. Music teachers are often guilty of staying in one place for the entire class time (behind the podium, in the front of the classroom, behind the piano, seated among the children). Teachers grow accustomed to the idea of the conductor on the podium. Listening to an ensemble from different vantage points, however, provides teachers with a comprehensive impression of the group's sound.

Shifting of location encourages students to remain alert and attuned to the musical experiences that occur in the rehearsal or classroom. In a general music class, the piano may be the most common magnet for a teacher and can become a barrier between the teacher and the students. Walking among the risers of a choir, among the students seated or moving during a general music class, or among different instrumental sections within a band or orchestra is a useful classroom management technique. It reminds students that the teacher is aware of all portions of a class or an ensemble.

Demonstration or modeling is the most common teaching technique and even has been found to increase the level of students' performance in comparison to a verbal-centered instruction (Dickey, 1991). During an observation, focus on those specific times when the teacher uses no verbiage but, rather, picks up an instrument to demonstrate articulation, phrasing, intonation, or an expressive nuance. During rehearsals, when does the choir director model the formulation of proper singing technique? During a general music class, when does a teacher demonstrate movement that accompanies a song?

Another worthy aspect of observation and recording is the musical content that is experienced by the learners. On which musical behaviors are the students and teacher focusing—composing, improvising, singing, playing, listening, moving, reading, describing, analyzing, critiquing? Are they learning about the historical and cultural contexts of the music or relating it to other subjects? What did the observer note that might serve as evidence of the students' musical learning? What strategies did the teacher implement in teaching or implementing the various student musical behaviors?

Since teaching is highly observable, videotape analysis is an excellent tool for evaluation. One can analyze lots of verbal—expression, inflection, enunciation, volume, clarity, variety—and nonverbal communicators—posture, eye contact, hand gestures, modeling, and movement in the room or proximity. When students first observe through the eyes of a teacher instead of a player, they gain a different understanding of the process of teaching. Varieties of teaching techniques become evident. Effectiveness of pace and delivery become important realizations. The art of teaching begins to unfold.

Techniques of Observing

To gain a broad view of any class or rehearsal setting, the most common style of collecting information is the **thick description**. As one collects "data" for an observation that culminates in writing a thick description, the observer acts like a sponge. She/he collects as much sensory information as possible and notes it in her/his journal. For instance, the description could include all activity, quotations, questions, physical descriptions of specific students and the teacher, the timbre of speaking voices, a diagram of the proxemics of the teacher to her/his students, body language, a description of the physical setting of the classroom or rehearsal space. Many of the scenarios that introduce each chapter of this text are types of thick descriptions. The more detail that is included in the report, the more holistic view the reader of the thick description has. A thick description is a flow of details and impressions that give information regarding classroom atmosphere and techniques. The resulting transcript provides a great amount of information that the observer can analyze to determine trends from student-teacher interactions. The narrative prose—the thick description—is full of vivid images, comparable to those found on a videotape that captures massive detail of a class or rehearsal.

Another observational technique, **question approach**, involves setting specific goals and stating questions that observers wish to have answered. These questions can include things such as the communication skills of the teacher and teaching techniques used. With questions to guide the observation, our sensory receptors are more focused on specific factors than while using the thick description method. How many times has a nervous mannerism of a speaker interfered with the message being presented? We can become easily distracted during the observation process if we are not guided by a specific objective. Making a form or a list of question-objectives on which to focus prior to observation assists in focusing the details being gathered during the observation.

In addition to an overview of a class, an observer may choose to make a list of specific actions or elements of a class or rehearsal that could be recorded in a systematic manner—**tally approach**. An example of this procedure is an observer who tallies the number of times the teacher stops the music-making in a secondary-level rehearsal. The observation record could involve keeping track of the number of times the teacher works with a section rather than the whole group or works on precision or rhythm or pitch. These segments can be given actual timed amounts by using the clock for the start and stop of each segment or by recording an observation every minute. This procedure provides the observer with specific information about the rehearsal that can be used for refining the specifics of the teaching process. Table 2.1 is an example of a format that can be used in recording the time that an identified aspect of the rehearsal is addressed. The percentage of the total rehearsal time can then be calculated.

Table 2.1　Tally/Timed Observation Table

Time	Topic 1 (rhythm)	Topic 2 (pitch)
1:00	0	violins
1:05	violas	0
1:10	entire group	0
1:15	entire group	0

The table indicates that the rehearsal began at 1:00 P.M. with the violins working on pitch, then the violas worked on rhythm, and then the entire group worked on rhythm. It is possible that there were other changes of topics and other sectional playing, but the recording time is an objective measure. The observation unit could be as large or as small as the observer wishes. The resulting information could be analyzed in timed units.

In another form of the tally approach, the observer could make a checklist of topics that might include melody, harmony, and rhythm, or in contest terms, precision, tone quality, dynamic contrasts, interpretation, technique, intonation. This method of observation is not only useful for observers of music instruction. Students in a music class or rehearsal can also keep track of musical concepts that they encounter by using such a checklist form.

Assignment: Thick Description

Goal: To observe presentation style, teaching, and musical skills of teachers in four different musical settings.

- Arrange to observe several music instruction settings (general music, chorus, band, orchestra) across the various age levels (preschool, elementary, middle school, high school).
- Plan to stay for the duration of the class/rehearsal. Be sure to arrive shortly before the class/rehearsal begins, so that your entry is not disruptive to the group.
- During the class/rehearsal, jot down detailed descriptions of the class/rehearsal environment, information about the class/rehearsal participants, and information about the presentational style, teaching strategies, questioning, and musical skills utilized by the instructors. *This is not an evaluation of the instructors' approaches to conducting the class/rehearsal!* Your task is to provide a "thick description" of details that you have absorbed through your senses.
- Following the observation, write a two-page, word-processed, essay description of the class/rehearsal you observed. Be descriptive! Be objective! Be interesting! You will be graded on the quality and accuracy of writing, content, and objective reporting of details from the class/rehearsal.

Assignment: Observation Questions

Goal: To focus on specific questions during the observation of a music instructional setting. Choose a few of the questions listed below on which you will focus your attention during the observation. Create a method for recording the information for each question (chart, checklist, narrative, thick description).

Observation Guidelines

I. **Quality of the rehearsal/classroom environment**
- Describe classroom/rehearsal space. Is it task-oriented, relaxed, or both?
- Describe physical attributes of the meeting space. Does it lend itself to learning and music-making?

II. **Teaching techniques**
How/when does the instructor use
- speaking?
- questioning?
- demonstration?
- verbal imagery?
- "visuals"?

III. **Teacher communication skills**
How/when does the instructor utilize
- movement in rehearsal/classroom?
- body gesture?
- facial expression?
- tone of voice?
- eye contact?
- other nonverbal communication?

IV. **Teacher musicianship**
How/when does the teacher show
- standards and expectations?
- expressiveness?
- knowledge of the music?
- correction of mistakes?
- positive feedback to the class/rehearsal participants?

V. **Participant responses**
Note the following:
- participants who are actively participating
- participants accomplishing musical goals
- interaction with other participants
- interaction with instructor

INTERVIEW

Think back to the "Most Influential Teacher" assignment at the end of the first chapter. What was the reason that this teacher was influential? Do you know why that person connected with you more than any other teacher? What might you learn from interviewing that person?

An interview, like an observation, is a technique that allows preservice music teachers and certified teachers to gather information about a person, a music situation, or the "secrets" behind the successes in teaching. The process of interviewing is similar to that of observing. First, decide what exactly you want to know about a specific person or music program. Then determine the best method for recording, organizing, and analyzing that information. Permission must be granted prior to an interview and prior to any audio- or videotaping that might occur during the interview.

What to Ask

Preservice teachers often have many questions about teaching in general and about specific choices that teachers make on a daily basis. There are many questions that one might ask of a teacher. Here is a list of questions that might lead to additional probing questions that are based on the teacher's response to the original questions. How did you get started in music? Who influenced you professionally? Why did you decide to study music education in college? How did you maintain your music performance interests while studying music education? How are you involved in the larger music education community? What sorts of experiences have shaped the teacher that you have become?

The information gathered from the interview can be recorded in a thick descriptive narrative or in a question-answer format. When considering the analysis of the information, the purpose of the interview comes into play. If the purpose of the interview is to gather data for a research project, then careful documentation of specific references would need to be noted. For example, a complete transcription from an audiotape would be necessary. A transcription includes notation of all pauses, laughter, vocal inflection and nuance, and explicatives. An example of a transcribed interview follows.

> Interviewer: So what were the main influences in your professional life?
>
> JK: Well, let's see (brief pause) . . . my mother was a third-grade public school teacher for thirty-four years, and she was an exemplary model for me. I was always playing school when I was a kid. I witnessed all the hard work my mother put into her work, and yet she continued to enjoy it. As for the music part, my church choir director and my high school choir director gave me my first opportunities to sing solos while I was an adolescent. I really felt the power of music as I performed, and that desire to perform and to teach music seemed like a perfect combination.

Interviewer: Did you ever feel as though that, by teaching, you had to forfeit your performing interests?

JK: Whew! A difficult question! (laugh). Until my mid-twenties, I *always* felt as though I had to decide between the two. If I performed too much, it would interfere with the energy I would have for my teaching and vice versa. Then I realized that I was fighting a battle that shouldn't be fought. Music teachers need to be competent practicing performers. Performance can occur in many different types of venues. If one is energetic and creative, one can have a career that includes performance and teaching. Again . . . a perfect combination.

If, however, the purpose of the interview is to procure background information, then the interviewee's responses to the interview questions could be paraphrased. A thick description, paraphrased narrative might be presented in the following manner, using the same information found in the transcribed interview format.

I met Ms. K. in a small, dark-lit coffeehouse on a snowy Friday afternoon. We were to meet at 3:30 P.M. (at the conclusion of her school day), but she was a bit late. The wind seemed to blow her in off of the street, as she apologetically, yet energetically, approached our table. She said that her rehearsal with a few students who were participating in the state solo/ensemble contest ran overtime.

Ms. K. looked a bit tired, but why not? It was the completion of a typically hectic week of a choral music education program at the high school level. She was very gracious in giving her time to meet with me.

I began the interview with a question that always interests me. I was most interested in how Ms. K. became involved in teaching music. She explained, in a pleasingly reminiscent manner, that her mother was an elementary school teacher for thirty-four years. Having a teacher for a mother gave her insight into the hard work, joy, and creativity that is involved in teaching. She also stated that her church choir director and her high school choral director gave her the opportunity to perform solos—the experience which ignited her passion for performing music.

It seems that only recently has Ms. K. come to terms with balancing her teaching responsibilities and her performing interests. Early in her studies and in her career, she thought that she had to choose between performance. She describes a career that combines performance opportunities with teaching as "a perfect combination."

Assignment: Interview

The following assignment allows the student new to music education to reflect on an influential teacher, to contact him/her, and to ask him/her some questions. This task can be instrumental in changing the way a student thinks about teaching. It has a positive impact on broadening the viewpoint of a first-year student who might become a prospective music educator.

Goal: To conduct a brief interview of a music educator (e.g., public school teacher, private/studio teacher, conductor) and write your findings in a brief report (suggested length: 1½ to 3 pages). Your interview may be conducted in person or via telephone.

Steps to Complete This Assignment

1. Think of a music educator you would like to interview for the assignment. Introduce yourself and explain the assignment to the potential interviewee; see if he/she is interested in participating and would be available for a five-to-fifteen-minute interview. Request permission in advance and make arrangements for a convenient time to conduct the interview.

2. Make a list of questions ahead of time, including some open-ended questions ("Tell me about . . . "). Here are some suggestions. Feel free to adapt any questions as needed or add your own ideas. You may need to "go with the flow" with new questions that evolve during the interview.

   - How long have you been teaching? At this age level? In this setting? Did you begin your career in your current position?
   - What aspect of teaching do you find most rewarding? Most inspiring? Most challenging? Most frustrating?
   - How do you organize and prepare for teaching? What strategies or systems do you find helpful?
   - Tell me about the support for your program. Is there community involvement? Parental involvement? Student involvement? Is it well supported by colleagues? Administrators? Tell me about the value of music education expressed by the principal and others.
   - How do you know that you "make a difference?"
   - What one piece of advice would you give to a student to assist in preparing for a music teaching career?

3. Be sure to thank your interviewee for his/her time. Followup with a thank you note.

4. Write your report and type it (word-process) using a standard twelve-point font, double-spaced, with 1- to 1½ inch margins. Add your own reflection to the interview in the final paragraph. (Perhaps one or more of the following: What did you find interesting? What did you find surprising? Did the person appear to value and enjoy his/her work? How did the interview impact your understanding of music education as a career?)

Assignment: Followup Discussion

When the interview assignment is completed, discuss what you found out about your teacher. We have found it effective to discuss these in a "kiva." This is a Southwestern Native American form of discussion in which people make a circle in a center or pit. A few, up to four, people are in the center of their own choosing. Only the people in the center may speak. The people in the large circle listen. Four desks are set up in the center; students come to those desks when they choose to talk about their interview. Students leave the center in their own time. This style of discussion brings a new dynamic to listening and focus. Silence plays an important role. The constant pressure to contribute to the discussion is relieved.

LESSON PLANNING

One major challenge for developing teachers is that of planning what they are to teach. A lesson plan is an outline that is useful for teachers and conductors in organizing the sequence of activity and questions asked during the lesson as well as the pace and delivery of material. A lesson might include not only the steps in teaching but also the items needed to teach. The lesson plan also should reflect the depth and breadth of the lesson content and the incorporation of the music content standards. Novice music educators often find it helpful to indicate the amount of time that will be devoted to each step in the lesson. Such detail and timing assist the teacher in focusing lesson segments, maintaining a directed lesson, and refraining from following tangents.

Although there are numerous effective lesson plan models, the following example reflects a lesson plan format that the authors choose to implement in their methods classes and in their own teaching. Key to developing a successful lesson plan is the understanding of developmental appropriateness, lesson sequencing, and the importance of students' active engagement. Sample lessons are found throughout this text.

LESSON PLAN FORMAT (REHEARSAL OR CLASSROOM)

I. **Grade Level**

II. **Musical Concept/Lesson Goal**

III. **Observable Learning Outcomes/Objectives**

 • Students will be able to . . .

IV. **Students' Prior Knowledge**

V. **National Standard(s) Addressed**

VI. **Materials Needed for Lesson (Student and Teacher)**

continued

VII.   **Teaching Procedures/Students' Active Engagement**

· Sequenced activities

· Transition statements and activities

· Questions!!!

· Transfer of learning/skills

· Anticipated length of each activity

VIII.   **Lesson Evaluation and/or Assessment**

What information is included in each section of this particular lesson plan format? The following provides a detailed dissection of each section of the lesson plan format.

I. **Grade Level**: The grade level and the specific class (general music, choral ensemble, orchestra, band, private lesson, sectional) for which the lesson is designed.

II. **Musical Concept/Lesson Goal**: That which is the musical focus of the lesson. Broad musical concept areas include style, steady beat, meter, rhythm, vocal style, pitch, steps and leaps, melodic contour, repetition and contrast, imitation, timbre, theme and variation, form, rondo, ABA form, monophony, polyphony, harmony, call and response, syncopation, pentatonic scale, chord progressions, intervals, cultural styles of music. The concept *area* should lead to a generalizable musical *concept* that is transferable to future music experiences such as, "Music can . . . [have a steady beat]" or "Music can . . . [be organized in ABA form]."

III. **Observable Learning Outcomes/Objectives**: The teacher's selection of one, two, or three musical behaviors or skills that the teacher can observe the students doing or performing, in order for the teacher to evaluate the success of the lesson and whether or not the goal of the lesson is attained. Objectives are most successfully observed when they are written using action verbs following the statement, "Students will be able to . . . " Some action verbs particularly relevant to music classes or ensemble settings include sing, play, harmonize, move, create, describe, listen, recognize, raise a hand, tap, hum, critique, evaluate, improvise, compose, read, and notate. Well-written objectives also assist the teacher in having the students constantly engaged in musical activity, rather than in a passive classroom environment.

IV. **Students' Prior Knowledge**: A list of information that the class or ensemble has learned in prior lessons and that serves as a foundation for all future lesson plans.

V.   **National Standards Addressed**: The musical behaviors and/or information used in the lesson that reflect the music content standards (and perhaps individual state standards for music instruction). [See National Standards for Music, in the Introduction.]

VI.   **Materials Needed for Lesson (Student and Teacher)**: A list of all materials that are necessary for a class or rehearsal (i.e., mallets, CD player, VCR, paper, chalkboard, CD title and track, charts, piano, etc.). Room setup also might be included in this section of the lesson plan.

VII.   **Teaching Procedures/Students' Active Engagement**: A sequenced plan, broken down into small pieces for learning, that is based on and that includes the observable learning behaviors (lesson objectives) listed in the beginning of the plan. Included in this section of the lesson plan are specific steps that lead the students to meaningful musical engagement, as well as means for having the students show that they can transfer understanding gained from one musical activity to another musical activity. Preservice music educators might wish to include a variety of scripted questions within each section of the procedure and transitional statements or activities that smoothly lead the students from one activity to another. An indication of time allotted for each step of the procedure might be a vital component of the procedure section, especially for novice music educators.

VIII.   **Lesson Evaluation and/or Assessment**: Written notes or other assessments made by the teacher about the degree to which the music students performed the observable learning outcomes (objectives) and ultimately the students' level of lesson goal/musical concepts mastery. Teachers use this section of the lesson to record that which was accomplished during the lesson and that which needs review or introduction during the next lesson. This section can also include those teaching strategies that were most effective and those that were less effective.

When prospective music educators observe experienced music teachers, especially in rehearsal settings, they may be puzzled when they do not see a written lesson plan or when they see a simple lesson plan block full of single words. Does the pithy description reflect a teacher's lack of planning? Not necessarily! Experienced, effective, and efficient music educators always follow written, or more frequently, mental lesson plans. Teachers' mental "rehearsal" of a lesson or rehearsal serves them well, because they are accustomed to being in front of students and are facile with appropriate music pedagogies and sequencing. Novice music educators and preservice music educators are strongly encouraged to develop skills in planning by creating detailed lesson plans.

Assignment: "How To . . . "

For this presentation, you should choose an activity that you can show us "how to do it." You will prepare a "lesson plan" to present this in five minutes. You will turn in this plan. This is similar to a lesson plan, but allows for more freedom in topics beyond and including music.

1. Goal—concept to teach (flower arranging)
2. Objectives—Students will . . . arrange four flowers in their vase according to principles of height, color, and distribution.
3. Materials needed—three vases, twelve flowers
4. Prepare the goal—demonstrate
5. Develop the skill—students do as asked
6. Transfer the skill—explain possibilities of arranging different flowers in different vases
7. Assessment—students' arrangements satisfy the objectives

SAMPLE LESSON PLAN

Grade: sixth grade general music

Musical Concept: repeated rhythmic pattern

Objectives: Students will be able to . . .

1. clap repeated rhythmic pattern

2. create notation, standard or invented, for a repeated rhythmic pattern

3. provide written description of changes that occur as rhythmic pattern is repeated (webbing)

Prior knowledge: standard rhythmic notation

National Standards: 4, 6

Materials: CD—Polynesian Drumming, "web" handout, stereo system, chalkboard, chairs moved to the sides of the classroom

Procedure:

1. Play recording of Polynesian Drumming (CD). Students will tap repeated rhythmic pattern when they identify it in the music.

2. Students will clap rhythmic pattern after listening example has been played.

continued

3. Students will create notation for the rhythmic pattern (standard or invented).

4. Have students draw on board their notation.

5. Repeat listening.

   Question: Even though the rhythmic pattern is the same, it changes. How? Write description in each of the web's ovals. Add more if necessary.

6. Discuss ways in which the same pattern can be changed so that repetition and contrast are created.

   Question: Any other possibilities for changing the rhythm (record student responses on chalkboard)?

Evaluation: Students need to experience finding repeated rhythmic patterns in additional pieces of music. Lesson objectives attained. I need to ask more focused questions prior to the listening of the examples.

JOURNALING

Maintaining a journal allows teachers and prospective teachers to reflect on what they saw and what they have said or taught, so that the next teaching/learning experience can be improved on. A journal is a tool necessary in developing preservice music educators' skills in reflection. Teachers who are reflective practitioners plan before they teach and then assess the successes and challenges that occurred during the execution of the lesson. Journals can be a way to let off steam after a difficult day or to celebrate a victory of something that was pedagogically effective. A journal might record an effective teaching strategy or a new revelation about one's life goals. A journal also might contain descriptions of students' reactions and responses during specific musical activity.

A class journal reflects preservice music educators' responses to topics discussed in class, topics to be discussed in class, questions about observations, or information gathered from other sources that directly relate to topics encountered in class. Journal entries can be about class content, or about something on a student's mind. A journal is a valuable method for communication between the teacher and student.

Assignment: Journal

Obtain a notebook for keeping journal entries. An entry will be made for each class, some topics assigned, other topics of your own choosing. Journals will be graded at midterm and at the end of the semester. Thoughtful entries and regular entries are important. Journals need to be typed or word-processed. All of the entries should be kept, so that by the end of the semester there are twenty-six entries. They can be as short as a paragraph, but the expression of a thought, the speculation about a topic or question, or the reflection of your development and interest in becoming a music educator are the crux of a meaningful and well-maintained journal.

Samples from Students' Journals

As I wrote in my paper on my interview, I gained much from this experience in two ways—not only did I learn about teaching, but I learned more about the expectations my professor has for students in his studio.

I love teachers. Each teacher has such a profound effect on the future. A teacher's knowledge is similar to an epidemic—when transmitted properly, it spreads like wildfire. Today's series of presentations increased my awareness of the teacher's importance in society. Not a single person in the class was apathetic concerning the influence their teacher has had in the outcome of their life thus far. That's commendable. At this point, I am in awe of the social power that the teacher holds. One teacher can severely slant a child's experience, either supporting or rejecting the child's interest. I believe a teacher holds more actual power than any group of politicians. (Although I will admit that the politician holds more concrete power, so far as legislation, etc.) I need however, to decide if I am worthy and energetic and idealistic enough to undertake the great responsibility of joining the education field. It seems very exciting, although challenging.

REFERENCES

DICKEY, M. (1991). "A Comparison of Verbal Instruction and Nonverbal Teacher-Student Modeling in Instrumental Ensembles." *Journal of Research in Music Education*, 39, pp. 132–42.

YARBROUGH, C. (1975). "Effect of Magnitude of Conductor Behavior on Students in Selected Mixed Choruses." *Journal of Research in Music Education*, 23, pp. 134–46.

3

Early Childhood Music Education

"Four minutes, four more minutes, and it will be Circle Time," Ms. E. along with her helpers, parents, and children at the Preschool Music Lab for 3-5 year-olds sing together to alert everyone that class is about to begin. The children scurry to different music stations in a hurry to try everything before Circle Time. I sit by the xylophones and play little melodies. Gus plops down next to me and looks expectantly at the mallets I have in my hand. "Are these yours?" I ask. I then put one mallet on either side of his head like antennae. "Do they go like this?" He laughs and shakes his head. I then hand him the mallets and he proceeds to play gingerly on the instrument. After a few seconds he finds another instrument across the room that holds new interest to him and away he goes. "Three minutes, three more minutes . . . " everyone sings. Next James sits down, grabs a pair of mallets and starts pounding away. He goes all the way up to the highest notes and all the way back down to the lowest. His face is very serious and focused on his masterpiece.

What is your earliest music memory? For many of you, it might be a lullaby sung for you to fall asleep, or perhaps songs on the radio to which you danced and clapped your hands. You may not have thought about these early experiences for a very long time.

As you contemplate a career in music education, it is helpful to think about the roots of your music experiences as a young child. Even if you do not ever teach music to young children, you will likely perform for them sometime in your career. Your teaching can be enhanced by knowing the music foundation skills appropriate for young children. The early childhood years are the most influential ones in our lives.

WHAT AGES ARE CONSIDERED "EARLY CHILDHOOD?"WHAT IS "DEVELOPMENTALLY APPROPRIATE" PRACTICE?

"Early childhood" is defined as birth through age eight by the National Association for the Education of Young Children (Bredecamp and Copple, 1997), the nation's largest professional organization of early childhood educators. The NAEYC states that "developmentally appropriate" early childhood programs are based on "what is known about how children develop and learn; such programs promote the development and enhance the learning of each individual child served" (p. 8). The organization recommends that at least three kinds of information be used for decisions regarding the well-being of children: (1) what is known about child development and learning; (2) what is known about the strengths, interests, and needs of each individual child in the group; and (3) what is known about the social and cultural contexts in which the children live. Collaborative decisions that take these dynamic and changing things into account constitute developmentally appropriate practice. The NAEYC describes specific principles for each of these three areas—human development and learning, individual characteristics and experiences, and social and cultural contexts—that inform developmentally appropriate practice. The Music Educators National Conference (MENC), our nation's largest professional music education organization, identifies National Standards for Music for early childhood/prekindergarten music experiences that take into account NAEYC guidelines for developmentally appropriate practice.

Early childhood settings begin with the home and may include childcare or daycare centers, other home care, preschools, and elementary schools with prekindergarten programs. Family members, however, are the primary caregivers of young children. Although family structures differ greatly, "caregivers become the first and most important music teachers for children" (Andress, 1998, p. 1). Music teachers can serve as resources in early childhood settings that do not have music specialists. Perhaps you have a young sibling, relative, or friend for whom you already provide additional music experiences.

The Young Child: Theory and Practice

Many of you probably have had some experience with young children. You may have observed some of the characteristics and behaviors that various theorists have described.

Young children learn through play. According to Jean Piaget (1952), children from birth through approximately age two (or when language begins) exhibit a **sensorimotor** stage of cognitive development, a prelanguage period dependent on physical and sensory experiences; children from age two to seven exhibit **preoperational thought**, characterized by language and conceptual development; seven- and eight-year-olds exhibit a stage of **concrete operations** in which they are able to apply logical thought to concrete problems. Lev Vygotsky (1978) also supported the importance of play as a way children learn but felt that learning was enhanced when adults and children interact. Adults, older children, and other "teachers" support children's learning by providing assistance, asking or answering questions, demonstrating, problem solving, or otherwise facilitating the acquisition of a new skill.

These are just two of the theories that can apply to musical characteristics and behaviors of young children. Other theories include those by Jerome Bruner, Maria Montessori, Howard Gardner, and Edwin Gordon; current early childhood curricula and materials include that by Barbara Andress, John Feierabend, Lynn Kleiner, Kindermusik, and Musikgarten, among others. Curricular issues, models, and approaches are described further by Jordan-Decarbo and Nelson (2002).

Going into a preschool or primary classroom with no idea how the children will react can be a daunting experience. Fortunately, children at each age or developmental level exhibit specific music behaviors (keeping in mind individual differences and overlapping of levels). The following examples are a few provided by Barbara Andress (1998); a more complete list can be found in her book.

The Musical Play and Behaviors of Young Children

Infants . . .
- enjoy being sung to while rocked or patted
- enjoy [gentle] bouncing motion
- respond happily to rhythmic play during body touch, singing, and chanting games
- respond to sound and often exhibit curiosity about where the song or sound is coming from
- participate in musical baby talk play
- enjoy the sounds of rattles, bells, and toys such as music boxes

Toddlers . . .
- create their own made-up songs
- combine bits of traditional songs with their own improvised songs
- are distinctly aware of musical and nonmusical sounds
- enjoy voice inflection games
- often display a delayed response during music time
- freely move to music
- are curious about sounds and shapes of all instruments

Three-year-olds . . .
- are more able to reproduce a recognizable song
- recognize the correct rhythmic and melodic contour of a song but cannot always reproduce what was heard
- enjoy manipulating hands-on play objects while creating songs
- enjoy repeatedly singing familiar songs
- move spontaneously to many styles of music
- play matching/classifying games
- can gallop, jump, run, and walk

Four-year-olds . . .
- demonstrate awareness of beat, tempo (fast-slow), volume (loud-soft), pitch (high-low), and form (same-different phrases)
- enjoy singing a wide variety of songs, and perform best when songs are within their singing range (D to A), but can also successfully sing songs in a more extended range (middle C-d' above second space c')
- can follow a guided musical story sequence
- use movement to describe distinct ideas heard in the music
- can identify the shape, size, and sound of classroom and some orchestral instruments

Five-year-olds . . .
- acquire a large repertoire of songs
- learn to play simple melodies on bells
- play instruments alone and in ensemble
- are increasingly more accurate with beat competency
- acquire understandings about basic music concepts
- delight in live performances and can identify various large performing groups

Six- to eight-year-olds . . .

· are able to understand introductory musical concepts about rhythm, melody, timbre, harmony/texture, expression, and articulation

· learn about music as they perform (sing and play instruments), describe (move and verbalize), and create (improvise and compose)

Excerpted from *Music for Young Children* (Andress, 1998, pp. 20–33)

Teaching examples for this (oldest) age group are included in Chapter 4.

CURRENT TEACHING APPROACHES WITH YOUNG CHILDREN

Sam comes marching in and over to the headphone listening area. This station allows children to identify sounds as they listen (to the ocean, animal noises, an orchestra, choir, rain, etc.) and point to a picture of things they are hearing. Sam was doing a pretty good job of this. It was interesting how his mother was listening as well, and encouraging him. Parent-child interaction is a must during this time. Another child, Josh, came into the room more reluctantly and wasn't sure he wanted to try any games or stations. His father coaxed him over to the xylophones. By this time, I was taken with this child and I stooped down to play the xylophones as well. His father and I would ask him to play a note and listen to whether that was higher or lower than the next note. Another child, Thomas, came over and joined the fun! He was most interested in the glockenspiels that "sound like a bell." The children can move to any station of their choice being creative and making music. The teacher circulates in the stations, sitting on the floor and helping out. The kids can have fun but learn, too, when an adult asks questions or suggests another option. There is plenty of excitement and enthusiasm in the class!

As more time passes, the teacher sings the "Five Minute" song:

Five min-utes!   Five more min-utes and it will be Cir-cle   Time. ___

This is a warning to the students that time in these stations is almost over and soon it will be Circle Time. By this time, most of the children have arrived and are working on various activities. After several more warning songs for the minutes remaining, it is at last Circle Time and the room is abuzz with change. Parents and student helpers scramble to move the instruments out of the way.

Each child is unique and develops at various rates with an overlapping of levels. A musical environment that is rich with opportunities and possibilities for exploration provides for differing learning styles and a variety of approaches. Since some children are not ready for cooperative play, for example, a curriculum consisting of only singing games is not developmentally appropriate practice.

Learning Centers or Stations

One way to provide for different types of play, individual interests, and developmental levels is to set up various "stations" or centers. These are simply areas that are grouped around a topic (a Train Center, Frog Center, or West African Center, for example), a musical skill or mode of engagement (a Singing Center or Movement Center, for example), or even a particular timbre (scraping or shaking instruments, drums, or bells). Within a given center, there may be opportunities for sorting objects, experimenting with sounds, listening, or performing other related activities. A Movement Center might have large plastic mirrors for children to watch themselves move, recorded music excerpts of many styles, scarves and other items for use as movement "props." Adults assist by describing or imitating movements made by the children and interacting with them.

Children freely come and go among the various centers during "Center Play." It can be very helpful in using Center Play with three- to five-year-olds to use a sung cue such as "Five minutes, five more minutes, and it will be Circle Time" sung on *So, Mi,* and *La* and repeated for four minutes down to one; this isn't because we expect the children to tell time (!) but to provide a structure for when Center Play will end and Circle Time will begin. Then, as children and helpers put all materials away, a separate song is used as we form our circle.

Circle Time!! A "let's make a circle" song is sung by everyone as children are seated. There are a few stragglers and the teacher sings, "Everybody to the circle by the count of three," expecting the children to scurry. They do. She grins and tells them there will be fun things to do today. We begin by passing the play microphone around and singing our name into it. Then the class has to sing it back in just the same way. It was great to see all these kids, even the shy ones, sing their name. It was an excellent activity for the students to hear the others sing, to recognize their voices. This became useful later on in the evening. Today's Circle Time was all about sounds and tone colors. The teacher demonstrated various instruments as the children moved to the sound of each. She held up cards with words and pictures such as clicking, ringing, scraping, shaking, or thumping. The class sang a song in which they guessed what percussion instrument was being played. Everyone got a turn in small

groups to play and to guess. The kids were very involved and excited about guessing. Next the children learned "Button You Must Wander," and the children guessed who had the button by the sound of their singing voice.

By utilizing a Center Play and Circle Time combination, more children's needs are met through more diverse ways of "knowing" about music.

Integrated Curriculum

The current interest in an integrated curriculum approach in early childhood education is appropriate to the learning style of this age group. Young children typically learn about their world in an integrated fashion, developing conceptual frameworks in large "chunks" rather than in isolated subject areas. An integrated curriculum utilizing music can allow for a collaborative instructional model that involves all teaching staff (not just the music specialist) working in conjunction with parents. Children develop autonomy as the "leader" in the exploration and discovery process, whereas the adults serve as facilitators that help describe and label the child's exploration efforts as well as entering into the play spontaneously themselves.

Materials for an integrated curriculum approach should have characteristics of all developmentally appropriate materials for early childhood education. They are stimulating, enticing, and of high quality—in short, they
are worthy of the child's valuable time. The materials should be rich in possibilities for exploration, manipulation, discovery, and, most important,
play. There is ample opportunity for interaction rather than "correctness"
and opportunity to facilitate the child's progress through learning cycles of
awareness, exploration, inquiry (an understanding of commonalities), and
utilization/manipulation.

Let us apply these characteristics to a specific integrated learning example using a musical concept by selecting a guideline set forth by the
NAEYC, namely, the need to provide "multicultural and nonsexist experiences" in early childhood curriculum. Our curricular theme can be Multicultural Music and Cultures for children ages four to seven. We will utilize
multicultural music and cultures within a "Tripartite Environment" as out-
lined by Andress (1998) and based in part on David Elkind's *Miseducation:
Preschoolers at Risk*. Such an environment includes three types of musical
presentation for learning: permeable learning (where music permeates the
day), special topic areas, and group music experiences. In this manner the
needs of all students can be met, because many might not be ready for *only*
group music experiences.

Multicultural music experiences are especially appropriate in early childhood, because the children's preferences and stereotypes have not yet been
formed, or are in the beginning stages of formation. Research by Elizabeth May
and Mantle Hood (1962) substantiates the need for multicultural music exposure to begin early.

Integrated Curriculum: An Example

Musical concept areas with a multicultural music focus in an integrated curriculum can be timbre and style. Group music time could utilize a "genre"
approach whereby song types that cross cultures are experienced: for example, lullabies, game songs (hiding a rock game, etc.), or work songs from,
for example, American Indian, African, and Latin American cultures. The
unique musical style of each culture's songs are highlighted. An audio- or
videotape of an authentic performance within each culture can be shared.
Learning these songs crosses several subject areas for integration, particularly language arts and social studies. In addition, counting songs sung in an
Indian language, an African language, and Spanish can be used to integrate
mathematics. All teaching staff and parents join the children for group
music experiences.

The permeable learning music segment of an integrated curriculum can
utilize multicultural music in a variety of ways. McCullough-Brabson (1993)

suggests using world music for transition times as a musical cue—in our example, American Indian flute music or African mbira (thumb piano) music can be used to signal nap time, for instance.

The third component of our integrative example can be special interest areas, particularly the use of centers. This is where the concept of timbre could really be emphasized. A Rattle Center could feature a variety of rattles—in our example, maracas for Latin American cultures, a shekere for African cultures (also could include a spin rattle and a basket rattle), and gourd rattles of various types for Pueblo Indian cultures. For an art project, the students could make container rattles out of cassette boxes, cans, or even ping-pong balls that had been drilled beforehand. Real gourds could even be grown, cut, and dried for making rattles.

A Drum Center could feature many types of drums from the selected cultures; again, students could make drums of their own. Another center could feature the Latin American guiro and the Yaqui notched rasp. Corrugated cardboard of various types could also be available for producing scraping timbres. Shaking or jingling timbres could be supplied in a center by Indian ankle bells for dancing, a tambourine, and an African forked rattle. (Ringing timbres could be supplied by a small Chinese gong and other instruments for a focus on China.)

In each center, tapes for listening and playing along could be included along with pictures of people within each culture playing the instruments. The pictures could feature both traditional and contemporary contexts.

A Dance Center can utilize movement "props" such as shawls, hoops, and ankle bells for dancing to Indian music, for example. Later, a videotape of Indian people dancing while using the materials could be included; however, imitation and exploration should be emphasized rather than replication or correctness. (The Dance Center could also include streamers and colorful ribbons on sticks that can be used with the Chinese Ribbon Dance, for example, with authentic photos of children performing.)

An Art Center can feature beads for stringing jewelry, clay for making pottery, or paper bags and paints to create cave wall petroglyphs. Appropriate pictures for each would be included, and parents or volunteers could be at each center to supervise and facilitate child-directed efforts.

A Singing Storyteller Center can be experienced with either a real person as the storyteller or, instead, a laminated playmat on which children could point to pictures and spontaneously improvise a sung story about Anansi the Spider (African) or Coyote (American Indian).

In addition to the three categories listed, guest artists and field trips help provide cultural context and additional learnings across the curriculum. Multicultural music can provide an exciting framework for an integrated curriculum that is child-centered and child-directed.

CLOSING THOUGHT

Music in the early childhood years provides a basis for all future music experiences. Young children delight in responding to music and sound. When a music environment is provided that is rich with opportunities to play, create, move, sing, listen, and otherwise explore, positive experiences with music result. "Such positive early experiences can give children a lifelong disposition toward music and musical learning—a gift truly worth giving" (Andress, 1998, p. 1). You will undoubtedly have many opportunities to share the gift of music with young children throughout your career.

SAMPLE SONGS AND TEACHING STRATEGIES

Teaching Strategy for Vocal Improvisation

For Center Play

Create a Singing Center with various objects such as puppets, play microphones (inexpensive echo microphones found at toy stores work well), play telephones (PVC "P" traps found at hardward stores work well), or singing tubes (empty gift wrap cardboard tubes, for example).

For Circle Time

Each child gets a turn (or may just pass) using one of the above objects to sing a greeting, their name, or anything else they wish. The rest of the class can echo.

Four Game Songs

Children ages four to eight will enjoy learning these game songs. Two songs are from Ghana, in West Africa; the third is from the Hopi, a Southwestern American Indian nation; and the fourth is from Zimbabwe.

Obwisana ("Ohb-wee-sah-nah")

- Teach song phrase-by-phrase in call and response or echo fashion, first by speaking, then singing.
- Use books such as *A Family in Ghana* by Lerner Publications (1985) to provide cultural context and to show pictures of children in Ghana today. Explain that children all over the world enjoy game songs. This song is often performed as a game of passing an object from one child to the next.

OBWISANA: FOLK SONG
(GHANA)

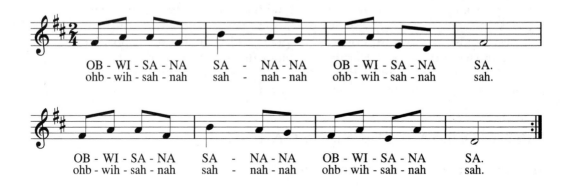

OB - WI - SA - NA   SA - NA - NA   OB - WI - SA - NA   SA.
ohb - wih - sah - nah   sah - nah - nah   ohb - wih - sah - nah   sah.

OB - WI - SA - NA   SA - NA - NA   OB - WI - SA - NA   SA.
ohb - wih - sah - nah   sah - nah - nah   ohb - wih - sah - nah   sah.

CHE CHE KOOLAY: GAME SONG
(GHANA)

Call and Response

CHE   CHE   KOO - LAY.   CHE CHE   KOO - FEE   SA.
[chay]

KOO - FEE SA LAN - GA.   KA - TA CHEE LAN - GA.   KOOM   A DAY DAY.

MOS', MOS'!
(HOPI, AMERICAN INDIAN)

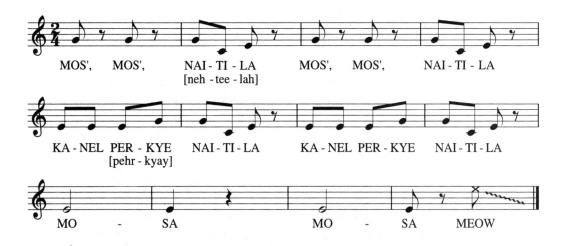

MOS',   MOS',   NAI - TI - LA   MOS',   MOS',   NAI - TI - LA
[neh - tee - lah]

KA - NEL PER - KYE   NAI - TI - LA   KA - NEL PER - KYE   NAI - TI - LA
[pehr - kyay]

MO - SA   MO - SA   MEOW

SORIDA: A SHONA HANDGAME SONG
(ZIMBABWE)

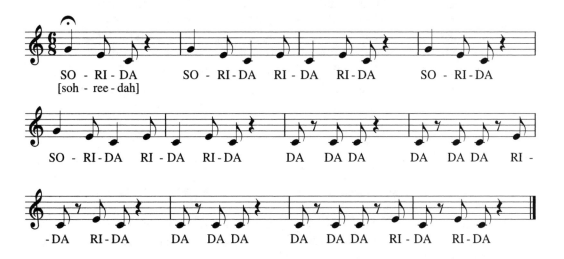

SO - RI - DA   SO - RI - DA   RI - DA   RI - DA   SO - RI - DA
[soh - ree - dah]

SO - RI - DA   RI - DA   RI - DA   DA   DA DA   DA   DA DA   RI -

-DA   RI - DA   DA   DA DA   DA   DA DA   RI - DA   RI - DA

- Explain that the words of "Obwisana" mean "Grandmother, I just hurt my finger on a rock."
- After learning the song, play a game of passing an object around the circle to the beat of the music. To do this, ask children to decide which hand will be their "passing hand" and to put that hand in front of their body with the other hand behind. Use "me, you" or "pick up, pass" to practice passing crumbled paper or another object to the beat.
  Extension: Use several of the same object, or enough objects for one/person.
- Recordings available: *The Music Connection*, grade 1—Silver Burdett Ginn
  Let Your Voice Be Heard—Judith Cook Tucker, World Music Press

Che Che Koolay *("Chay chay koolay")*

- Teach song phrase-by-phrase in call and response or echo fashion, first by speaking, then singing.
- Use books such as *A Family in Ghana* (Lerner Publications, 1985) to provide cultural context and to show pictures of children in Ghana today. Explain that children all over the world enjoy game songs. This song is often done as a game of "follow the leader."
- Explain that the words to this song are like "tra la la," but may have been parts of words in a language used long ago.
- These actions are often used with this song: Phrase 1—tap head to the beat; Phrase 2—tap shoulders to the beat; Phrase 3—tap hips to the beat; Phrase 4—tap knees to the beat; Phrase 5—jump in place on "Koom" with hands on hips. After singing twice through, add "Hey!" at the end of song and "freeze." Divide class in half; one half does the "call" and the other the "response." Switch. Extension: First and second graders can create body motions for one phrase each in small groups or individually; take turns with new leaders.
- Recordings available: *Smorgasboard*—Sharon, Lois, and Bram
  The Music Connection, grade 1—Silver Burdett Ginn
  Let Your Voice Be Heard—Judith Cook Tucker ("Kye Kye Kule")

Mos' Mos' *("Mohss, mohss")*

- Teach song phrase-by-phrase in call and response or echo fashion, first by speaking, then singing.
- Use books such as *A New True Book: The Hopi* by Ann Heirichs Tomchek (Children's Press, 1987), to provide cultural context and to show pictures of children in Hopiland today. Explain that children all over the world enjoy game songs. This song is a kind of game that also tells a story about a cat

(perhaps a mountain lion) that steals a sheepskin. The words are from both the Hopi and Navajo languages.

· At the end, children will enjoy turning to their neighbors and using catlike arm motions to match the downward vocal "meow" sounds.

Extension: Add Hopi gourd rattles to fit the rhythm of the words; at the end, shake the rattles.

· Recordings available: *The Music Connection*, grade 1—Silver Burdett Ginn
Multicultural Perspectives in Music Education—Music Educators National Conference (MENC)

Sorida ("Soh-ree-dah")

· Teach song phrase-by-phrase in call and response or echo fashion, first by speaking, then singing.
· Use books such as *A Family in Zimbabwe* (Lerner Publications, 1985), to provide cultural context and to show pictures of children in Zimbabwe today. Explain that children all over the world enjoy game songs. This song is often performed as a game of getting faster and faster.
· Explain that the words to this song are from the Shona people, and mean "Hello" or "Shalom," this is a greeting song as well as a type of game song.
· These actions are often used with this song: Arms circle up and around on "So-ri-" and hands clap together on "-da." Make very small circles on "ri-da, ri-da," again clapping on "-da" each time.

Extension: Sing gradually faster and faster each time, or gradually faster throughout the song.

· Recordings available: *The Music Connection*, grade 1—Silver Burdett Ginn
Let Your Voice Be Heard—Judith Cook Tucker, World Music Press

QUESTIONS FOR DISCUSSION

1. What is your earliest music memory?
2. What experiences have you had working with children? What kinds of musical and learning behaviors have you already encountered?

FOLLOWUP ACTIVITIES AND ASSIGNMENTS

1. Observe young children whenever possible for one week—at a childcare center, mall, church, school, or sports event. Keep a journal of the children's spontaneous musical behaviors. Include the locations and the amount of time spent at each. Compile and thoroughly describe your findings.

2. Design and create a Music Center based on information provided in this chapter. Make sure that all materials in your center are safe for use by young children. Observe and interact with children as they use your center. If time allows, make needed modifications and use again. What did children enjoy about your center? What did they learn and experience?

3. Select an article from the July 1999 issue of *Music Educators Journal* (Special Focus: Music and Early Childhood). Review and discuss. What applications can you make for your future teaching?

REFERENCES

ANDRESS, B. (1998). *Music for Young Children*. Fort Worth, TX: Harcourt Brace College Publishers.

ANDRESS, B. and WALKER, L. (eds.). (1993). *Readings in Early Childhood Music Education*. Reston, VA: MENC.

ANDERSON, W. and CAMPBELL, P. (eds.) (1996, second ed.). *Multicultural Perspectives in Music Education*. Reston, VA: MENC.

BREDEKAMP, S. and COPPLE, C. (eds.). (1996) *Developmentally Appropriate Practice in Early Childhood Programs* (rev. ed.). Washington, DC: National Association for the Education of Young Children.

ELKIND, D. (1987). *Miseducation: Preschoolers at Risk*. New York: Alfred A. Knopf.

GRIFFIN, M. (1985). *A Family in Ghana*. Minneapolis, MN: Lerner Publications Co.

GRIFFIN, M. (1985). *A Family in Zimbabwe*. Minneapolis, MN: Lerner Publications Co.

JORDAN-DECARBO, J. and NELSON, J. (2002). "Music and Early Childhood Education." In Colwell, R. and Richardson, C. (eds.), *The New Handbook of Research on Music Teaching and Learning*. New York: Oxford University Press/MENC: The National Association for Music Education.

MAY, E. and HOOD, M. (1962, April–May). "Javanese Music for American Children." *Music Educators Journal*, 48, pp. 38-41.

MCCULLOUGH-BRABSON, E. (1993). "Early Childhood Multicultural Music Education." In Andress, B. and Walker, L. (eds.), *Readings in Early Childhood Music Education*. Reston, VA: MENC.

PIAGET, J. (1952). *The Psychology of Intelligence*. Trans. Percy, M. and Berlyne, D. E. London: Routledge and Kegan Paul.

The Music Connection. (1995). Morristown, NJ: Silver Burdett Ginn, Inc.

The Music Connection. (2000). Parsippany, NJ: Silver Burdett Ginn/Scott Foresman.

TOMCHEK, A. (1987). *A New True Book: The Hopi*. Chicago, IL: Children's Press.

TUCKER, J. (1993 and 2002). *Let Your Voice Be Heard!* Danbury, CT: World Music Press.

VYGOTSKY, L. (1978). *Mind in Society: The Development of High Psychological Processes*. Cambridge, MA: Harvard University Press.

Valuable Internet Resources

Music Educators National Conference (MENC) <www.menc.org>; MENC has an Early Childhood Special Research Interest Group and many publications on early childhood music education.

National Association for the Education of Young Children <www.naeyc.org>.

4

General Music in the Elementary School

Matthew, a music education major, was observing several music classes in an elementary school as part of his junior fall semester methods course and writing observations and questions in his journal. So far, Matthew had enjoyed his observation of a fifth-grade general music class but found himself somewhat baffled. Thinking back on his own school music classes in fifth grade, all Matthew could remember was singing "Erie Canal" out of a book while the teacher accompanied the class on piano. That was fun but very different from what he was currently observing.

Matthew noted in his journal his surprise that fifth graders could perform an arrangement for the Mexican marimba on Orff xylophones, complete with Latin percussion. As all the students sang in Spanish, some were playing instruments, while others moved to the "cha-cha" rhythm patterns. The class learned the formal structure of the piece, the meaning of the words, and information about Mexican marimba ensembles in general. Everyone in the class participated and was involved, although Matthew observed that some students appeared to be more "on task" than others. Several students performed only simple repetitive patterns; others performed more complex patterns.

Matthew wondered how and why the teacher had chosen certain parts for certain students, or whether the process was random. For that matter, how did the teacher know which repertoire was appropriate or "do-able" for fifth grade?

As Matthew sat there absorbing the lesson's closure, the general music teacher led the next class, a kindergarten, into a circle while everyone sang a song. The teacher used a hand puppet as the children were invited to join in "singing conversations" with the puppet. Although Matthew thought that the lessons might focus on pitch using vocal improvisation, to the children it seemed more like some fun music activities. Next, the teacher taught two songs in a phrase-by-phrase echo fashion using *So* and *Mi*. Matthew vaguely remembered a National Standard involving singing from his methods class . . . and wondered if it was difficult for the music teacher to "switch gears" from teaching fifth grade to kindergarten in back-to-back lessons.

As the kindergarten class finished, a fourth-grade class was already waiting at the classroom door. There was some confusion as the students got out their own recorders although the class appeared to be familiar with the procedures. After some echo playing led by the teacher, students were given time to improvise a melody using B, A, G, E, and their new note, D. The teacher used a "question-answer" phrase format to hear each student's melody. Matthew saw the teacher jot down something on a laminated seating chart as each student played. The class then reviewed the term "pentatonic" and learned a new pentatonic piece from written notation, first counting the rhythm with *ta*s and *ti*s. The teacher said that next time the students would get to listen to a Native American flute piece that was pentatonic.

As Matthew was leaving the classroom he glanced at the teacher's schedule and noticed that a first-grade class would be coming in next. How did the teacher plan for teaching each different grade level? How did the teacher keep track of so many different classes and what they were working on?

In these three classes, Matthew had observed singing, playing, moving, and improvising. Matthew knew from his coursework and listening carefully to the teacher's presentation that there were music concepts and National Standards for Music on which the lessons were based. The teacher was busy with the variety and needs of the various classes, grade levels, and individual children. Yet, Matthew noted that teacher and students alike apparently enjoyed music classes, and that students were given opportunities to "discover," demonstrate, and often verbalize their learning throughout the lessons. He had lots of questions and comments to bring up in his next methods class.

WHAT IS "GENERAL MUSIC?"

Matthew had observed a fairly typical segment of an elementary general music teacher's day. Although some elementary schools include sixth grade, a K–5 (kindergarten through fifth grade) or preK–5 (prekindergarten through fifth grade) framework is common.

But what is "general music?" From the sound of it, "general" could refer to vague dabbling in a "nonspecific" area of music study—just music "in general," for whoever wants to learn. For this reason the term "general" is often problematic for music educators. In spite of what the term "general" implies, "general music" can be defined productively as *the comprehensive study of music for all students.*[1]

Let's examine this definition more closely by looking at each component separately. First, "comprehensive" implies a broad study of music through a variety of means—singing, playing, moving, listening, creating, describing, and relating music to other areas of learning. These "-ing" words are ways general music teachers—and other music educators—engage students through active or "hands-on" learning of music skills. The concept areas or elements of music—pitch, duration, texture, form, timbre, and expressive qualities—are experienced through the "modes of engagement," or skills, such as singing, playing, listening, and so on. Concepts are typically "revisited" in each grade level in a more complex manner in a spiral curriculum fashion.

"Comprehensive" also implies a balanced and sequential curriculum. Careful, sequential planning elevates general music from an activity-driven

---

[1]Definition shared by Jacquelyn Boswell; source unknown.

or product-oriented curriculum to one based on music outcomes, goals, and standards. "Process" is balanced with "product" to suit children's learning needs in age-appropriate ways. Elementary general music curricula often emphasize "process" over "product" to provide all children opportunities for musical creativity without undue performance pressures. Finding a balance is key.

Next in our definition is the phrase "for all students." General music classes provide experiences for *every* child in an elementary school—not just for those children who choose (or have been chosen) to be in a performing group, or those with the financial means or opportunity for private music study.

Although general music is taught at many levels—prekindergarten/early childhood, elementary, middle and high school or even adults—we will limit our discussion to elementary music in K–5 school settings. Keep in mind that general music teachers/specialists often have choirs or choruses; these teachers are sometimes referred to as "general/choral" music teachers or specialists. General music is usually offered in public schools, private schools, and other types of school settings such as magnet and charter schools, although the frequency of general music instruction (twice per week, once per week, once every other week) can vary greatly.

THE ELEMENTARY STUDENT:
THEORY AND PRACTICE

In the scenario described at the beginning of this chapter, Matthew wondered how the music teacher knew "at what age children could do what." In other words, what specific music behaviors can be expected—what are children capable of musically—and at what age?

To answer this question, first we must ask, "Who are the students in elementary schools and what developmental characteristics describe elementary school students?" In most cases, children ages five to eleven attend K–5 elementary schools—although some schools may include a prekindergarten and others include sixth grade. Other school systems separate the grades K–2 (primary) and 3–5 (intermediate) or K–3 and 4–6. Special-needs and gifted students are typically mainstreamed into the general music classroom—that is, these students typically attend music class with their regular "homeroom" class.

A wide span of developmental levels are present from ages five to eleven. The work of various learning theorists, only a few of which are included here, applies to teaching elementary students. Although a very brief overview follows, you will most likely be learning more about these theories in future courses. As mentioned in Chapter 3, Jean Piaget (1952) identified the following stages of cognitive development that apply to elementary-age children: preoperational thought (approximately age two to seven, affecting especially K–2), the concrete operations stage (approximately age seven to eleven, or grades 2–5), and formal operations (beginning approximately age eleven, or grade 5). Developmentally appropriate practice based on the work of Piaget and others justifies the need for lots of sensory-based, concrete experiences in which young children learn by doing, saving the activities requiring abstract reasoning for fifth grade and later.

Jerome Bruner (1966) identified enactive, iconic, and symbolic modes of representation. For example, children could first move to the rhythm of "Yankee Doodle" (enactive) then use short and long lines to show the rhythm of the song (iconic), then use the standard notation for "Yankee Doodle" (symbolic). Bruner advocated a "discovery method" of learning within a spiral curriculum in which concepts are "revisited" in more complex ways as children mature. For example, first graders and fifth graders might both be working on keeping a steady beat; however, first graders might pat their bodies to the steady beat of a Sousa march, whereas fifth graders might work on groupings of the steady beat in a meter of seven while they listen to Dave Brubeck's "Unsquare Dance."

You have probably heard of Howard Gardner (1983), who developed a theory of multiple intelligences that identifies music as a separate intelligence.

The inclusive environment of a general music class facilitates multiple ways of "knowing" about music.

Have you noticed that you learn certain types of material better visually, aurally, or kinesthetically, through moving? Or perhaps, as a musician, you blend seeing, hearing, and sensing through movement—for example, the "muscular memory" of your hands knowing how to perform a piece for piano by memory combined with hearing the piece and visualizing it on the printed page. We *all* have exceptionalities and ways we learn best. General music can meet the needs of all learners by providing many ways to learn, which includes making adaptations to fit the abilities of special-needs students. Elementary-age children typically learn by seeing, hearing, touching, moving, exploring, and manipulating objects in their environment as part of their preoperational thought and concrete learning. For this reason, an environment rich with creative possibilities and opportunities provides multiple ways for children to learn.

How do these characteristics translate into music behaviors? One example of expected music outcomes, behaviors, or goals for each grade level is provided by Anderson and Lawrence (2001). Note how the stages identified by Piaget and Bruner are reflected in these musical behaviors:

Developing Objectives—Expected Musical Behaviors

Preschool/Kindergarten

Students will:
1. Sing short songs in tune, with good breathing habits and tone quality.
2. Perform rhythms with a steady beat.
3. Perform music expressively.
   a. Loud-soft
   b. Fast-slow
   c. Legato-staccato
4. Respond to expressive qualities of music through movement.
   a. Duple meter and triple meter
   b. Strong accents and changing accents
   c. Steady beat
   d. Changing dynamics
5. Play simple rhythmic-melodic patterns on classroom instruments.
6. Sing, play, move, and create music expressive of individual imaginations.

Grades 1 and 2

Students will:
1. Sing short songs in tune, with good breathing habits and tone quality.
2. Distinguish between high and low, fast and slow, and instrumental tone colors.
3. Identify expressive use of repetition and contrast in simple songs and short listening examples.
4. Express through creative movement such musical concepts as:
   a. Steady beat
   b. Accent
   c. Gradually getting louder or softer
   d. Staccato
   e. Legato
5. Engage in singing games.
6. Play simple rhythmic-melodic patterns on classroom instruments.
7. Read and create simple music notation.

Grades 3 and 4

Students will:
1. Sing short songs in tune, with good breathing habits and tone quality.
2. Sing simple rounds and descants in tune.

3. Sing songs expressive of text.
   a. Legato and staccato
   b. Dynamics
   c. Phrasing
4 Analyze music in terms of elements.
   a. Melodic phrases
   b. Tone colors
   c. Formal structure
5. Read or create simple music notation.
6. Engage in singing games and dances.
7. Play simple melodies and rhythmic accompaniments on classroom instruments.

Grades 5 and 6

Students will:
1. Sing songs in tune, with good breathing habits and tone quality.
2. Sing songs in two and three parts.
3. Demonstrate rhythmic sense through:
   a. Identifying simple-to-complex rhythms (both verbally and aurally)
   b. Playing rhythms in 2/4, 3/4, 6/8, mixed meter
4. Play simple harmonic accompaniments on guitar, keyboard, or Omnichord [QChord].
5. Play simple melodies and descants on melody bells or recorder.
6. Identify music from other parts of the world according to its use of melody, rhythm, texture, tone color, and formal structure.
7. Develop musical leadership by taking part in musical plays.
8. Read and write music notation.

From *Integrating Music into the Elementary Classroom,* Fifth Edition, Wadsworth/Thomson Learning, Inc., © 2001, pp. 23–24.

Elementary school children not only exhibit various developmental levels and ways of learning but also display diversity with regard to a whole range of exceptionalities and cultures. General music can provide highly successful experiences for all students. Here is a journal entry from a student teacher:

> In a few of our classes I have some handicapped children who are mainstreamed and are in the music classroom with us. One in particular is Erin, a Down's syndrome child who is nine or ten and in the first grade for the third or fourth year. I have been observing her to see how she relates to music and I was pleased with the results. Rhythms seem not to be a problem, but she has not successfully accessed her head voice yet. She

has an aid who comes to class regularly and helps her out. I have tried to notice how Mrs. G. includes Erin in the class by using her ideas . . . it is a different experience to be a part of a real classroom and interact with these children; we talk about mainstreamed children in methods classes but it is really different when you are actually teaching.

AN OVERVIEW OF THE HISTORY OF GENERAL MUSIC IN AMERICAN MUSIC EDUCATION

General music is a part of most elementary schools' curricula. How did this come about? The value of music instruction as part of a curriculum of study dates back to the Greeks, but we shall concern ourselves here with only the American history of music education and the instructional needs it served for its time. Although some of the people and events will also be covered in various other chapters of this book, a historical overview as it relates to general music is helpful here.

Prior to 1800, music primarily served religious needs for settlers in America. In 1838, Lowell Mason began the first school music program in Boston. Some of the principles he applied are still used today—sound before sight, theory follows practice, and active learning—but students learned about music only by singing. The religious, moral, and physical justifications for having music in the curriculum continued into the early 1900s. Singing, music theory, and music appreciation were important focuses of the music curriculum. A man by the name of Tomlins advocated the importance of developing one's aesthetic nature. Although this justification was not readily embraced in its time, much later it would become a vital reason for the inclusion of music in school curriculum. The early 1900s marked the child-study movement and the beginning of progressive education, a philosophy of such educators as John Dewey.

During the period of 1917–42, many changes took place. Although singing and sight-singing were still important components of music curriculum, correlations to other subject areas took on greater importance. Today we call these "extramusical" justifications for music in the school—for example, the development of breath control, coordination, and moral character—justifications even used by Lowell Mason much earlier. There was also an interest in tests and measurements, resulting in the first music aptitude/achievement tests by music psychologist Carl Seashore. The invention of the phonograph and its increased popularity, along with the popularity of the radio, also influenced school music activities. Listening and listening contests were added to the curriculum. Movement, folk dance, and Dalcroze Eurhythmics also were added, particularly in elementary music curriculum. Instrumental music instruction began as well; class piano was popular in the 1920s and 1930s. The philosophy of progressive education played an important role in music instruction. The phrase, "Music for every child, every child for music," coined by Karl Gehrkens in 1923, is still a guiding principle for the music education profession and is particularly applicable to general music contexts. The writings of James Mursell, a music psychologist, greatly influenced music teachers to emphasize the *process* or experience rather than the *product* in their teaching. A Gestaltist, Mursell believed in educating the whole child and is sometimes referred to as the "grandfather of general music education."

Great changes were on the way, for the period of 1942–67 resulted in the demise of progressive education. The launch of Sputnik brought with it an unprecedented emphasis on science and the intellect, leaving an indelible mark on education—music education included. As a result, there was greater emphasis on the intellectual and entertainment value of music. Psychology also became important; the work of Jean Piaget and Jerome Bruner affected music education in particular. Theirs was a developmental approach to teaching and curriculum design that is still used today. The influence of behavioral psychology resulted in an emphasis on *doing* that also remains today.

Classroom music activities further expanded to include not only singing but playing instruments, moving, creating, listening, and reading music. Music methodologies or approaches such as Orff and Kodály were adopted and adapted in North America (although previously in Europe) during this time. There was a "basic concepts revolution" accompanied by emphases on individuality and accountability. Federal funding for the arts was at its peak. There were many important events in the music education profession during this time. The Tanglewood Symposium, for example, resulted in the Tanglewood Declaration, which called for music to be placed at the core of the curriculum. The formation of the Rockefeller and Ford Foundations, the National Endowments for the Arts and Humanities, as well as many other federally funded organizations and events such as the Contemporary Music Project (followed by the Comprehensive Musicianship Project, from which the concept of Comprehensive Musicianship evolved) and the Manhattanville Music Curriculum Project (MMCP) were influential during this period.

The changing values of youth that were evident in the 1960s resulted in apathy toward education and the arts during the next period, 1967 to the mid-1990s and perhaps to the present day. Schools were (and are) attacked for not being effective with an ever-increasing emphasis on accountability. Americans became more passive, satisfied, and pleasure-seeking. Diversity became an issue relevant to education in the 1980s and 1990s, marked by professional events such as the Wesleyan Symposium of 1984 and the 1990 Symposium on Multicultural Approaches to Music Education. Methodologies such as Kodály, the Orff Process, and Dalcroze evidenced a revival as curricular approaches. There was an explosion of ideas and technology.

In 1993, a symposium on "new visions for general music" was held by the Society for General Music and MENC (Stauffer, 1995). Charles Leonhard articulated the need for music as part of an aesthetic education around 1967. Others such as Bennett Reimer have expounded on it since. An aesthetic education involves a way of knowing about the arts and, through the arts, knowing about how life feels. Today we see our job as music educators as one involving a responsibility to elicit aesthetic response and behaviors from our students through their active involvement with music as art. Through their experience with music, students discover its joy.

CURRENT TEACHING APPROACHES IN K–5 GENERAL MUSIC

Current general music curricula in the elementary school reflect the *National Standards for the Arts*, published by Music Educators National Conference (MENC, 1994) for preK–12. As described in the Introduction of this book, each of the nine voluntary content standards has correlating achievement standards. A given school's curriculum is based on national, state, and district guidelines. Music teachers/directors select and design their lessons or rehearsals based on goals, outcomes, concepts, and objectives influenced by a personal philosophy of music education.

In the general music classroom, one or more concept areas (for example, pitch, duration, form) are typically the focus of a lesson. A "concept" is something learned from the lesson about a musical element—a "residual" or generality—that can be reapplied to something new, for example, "Music can have a steady beat." A behavioral objective states an action children will do such as, "Students will be able to create body movements to match the steady beat of the selected music." Current basal music textbook series adopted by most states such as Silver Burdett Ginn's *Making Music* (published by Scott Foresman/Pearson Group, 2002) or *The Music Connection* (published by Scott Foresman/Silver Burdett Ginn, 1995 and 2000) or McGraw-Hill/Macmillan's *Share the Music* (1995) and a forthcoming new edition of the latter text provide lesson plans and sequential guides for teaching musical concepts or other thematic ideas. Here is a student teacher's description of his lesson concept:

> My concept development for the lesson was ABA form . . . we did the Bluebird song twice and between each time there was a chant/improvising opportunity for the students. I had students come up each time to improvise at the xylophone on the B section. We then took colored shapes and identified each section with triangles and circles; this was followed by labeling each shape with an A or a B.

Many general music teachers with an "eclectic" background select a teaching approach to correlate with an objective in an age-appropriate way that best meets the students' needs while other teachers specialize in one or more teaching approaches. Of these, three major approaches are described here. Additional information is provided at the end of this chapter.

Orff-*Schulwerk*[2]

Based on the ideas of the German composer Carl Orff (1895–1982), Orff-*Schulwerk* ("schoolwork") is a *process* that "begins where the child is," utilizing rhymes, chants, and songs. In America, the Orff Process consists of imitation, exploration, literacy, and improvisation (Campbell and Scott-Kassner, 2002). In the Orff Process, "speech play" or rhythmic speaking is often used as a starting point with "body percussion"—clapping, snapping, stomping, and patting ("patsching"). The body percussion parts are then transferred to un-pitched percussion instruments and later transferred to pitched mallet instruments such as xylophones, metallophones, and glockenspiels. The child is typically doing more than one thing simultaneously (for example, singing while playing a rhythmic pattern). Movement is an important aspect of Orff-*Schulwerk*, as is improvisation.

Kodály[3]

Based on the ideas of the Hungarian composer Zoltan Kodály (1882–1967), this approach utilizes folk song material. Sequential learning is important; there is a specific *melodic sequence* that begins with *So* or *Sol-Mi* using singing, solfège, and Curwen hand signals and a *rhythmic sequence* that begins with "ta" for quarter notes and "ti-ti" for eighth notes. The development of inner hearing, listening, and performance skills enables all children to read and write music. Music literacy is emphasized as a goal of this approach in which "music belongs to everyone."

Dalcroze[4]

Based on the ideas of the Swiss music educator Emile Jaques-Dalcroze (1865–1950), this approach is comprised of ear training/solfège, improvisation,

---

[2]The professional organization founded on Orff's ideas is the American Orff-*Schulwerk* Association (AOSA), which has state chapters nationwide. This association organizes a national conference yearly and numerous Saturday workshops sponsored by local chapters. The organization's journal is *The Orff Echo*. There are three levels of certification and masterclasses in Orff-*Schulwerk*. Important resources include the five volumes of *Music Fur Kinder* published by Schott, the three "American" volumes entitled *Music for Children* published by Schott, *Discovering Orff* by Jane Frazee, and *Exploring Orff* by Arvida Steen (AOSA National Office: P.O. Box 391089, Cleveland, OH 44139; http://www.aosa.org).

[3]The professional organization founded on Kodály's ideas is the Organization of American Kodály Educators (OAKE), which has state chapters nationwide. This association also organizes a national conference that alternates with regional conferences yearly and numerous Saturday workshops sponsored by local chapters. The organization's journal is *The Kodály Envoy*. There are four levels of certification in Kodály training. Important resources include *The Kodály Method I* and *The Kodály Method II* by Lois Choksy. There is also a Kodály text for early childhood entitled *Music in Preschool* by Katalin Forrai (translated by Jean Sinor) (OAKE National Office: 1612 29th Avenue South, Moorhead, MN 56560; http://www.oake.org).

[4]The professional organization founded on Dalcroze's ideas is The Dalcroze Society of America, which has chapters nationwide. National conferences and local workshops are offered. Certification and licensure courses are available in the summer. Resources include texts by Robert Abramson or Virginia Hoge Mead such as *Dalcroze Eurhythmics in Today's Music Classrooms* published by Schott and *The Rhythm Inside* by Black and Moore (http://www.dalcrozeusa.org).

and eurhythmics. Of these, Dalcroze Eurhythmics is most widely incorporated in the elementary general music classroom. In this approach, the body is an instrument that expresses any aspect of the music. The teacher often improvises at the piano; however, other instruments, recorded music, and many other means also are used. Teaching techniques include games and principles such as "follow" and "quick change."

Other teaching approaches utilized in elementary general music that you may learn about in future courses include the Manhattanville Music Curriculum Project (MMCP), Comprehensive Musicianship (CM), and Gordon's learning theory.[5] Additional techniques from the general field of education such as cooperative learning (a type of small-group learning) are employed successfully in the elementary music class (Kaplan and Stauffer, 1994). Technology is also a teaching tool in general music; for instance, the computer program entitled *Making Music*, by Morton Subotnick, allows children to create compositions and notate them iconographically with pictures. Many teachers choose to blend various approaches to match their own interest and expertise, lesson objectives, and students' needs. Teaching K–5 general music is a challenging task that offers variety and creativity for teacher and students alike.[6]

ASSESSMENT AND EVALUATION

General music teachers can evaluate and assess student learning in diverse ways. Although student participation is one indicator of student involvement and learning there are many other means of documenting student progress through observation, videotape, audiotape, journals, compositions, portfolios, and tests. Here is a student teacher's description of an assessment and its rubric used by his cooperating teacher:

> On the first lesson of the week, we had to do assessments. One of the objectives for this quarter was for students to be able to write rhythm patterns using "ta" and "ti." For the first lesson we used popsicle sticks to show the patterns and Mrs. G. went around to assess which students could do it. The other assessment in the first lesson was keeping a steady beat; we used a song they had been working on with the Orff instruments and the students kept the beat on one of the instruments while the class sang and Mrs. G. assessed. She kept track of everything in her grade book, marking a "+" for "can do all the time," a check for "most of the time," and a "–" for "not yet."

---

[5]Edwin Gordon (b. 1928) founded the Gordon Institute of Music Learning (GIML), which offers two levels of certification in general music and instrumental music. Resources include *Jump Right In*, published by GIA (GIA Publishing) and Gordon's *Learning Theory*.

[6]Another helpful resource for the reader is Campbell and Scott-Kassner, *Music in Childhood: From Preschool through the Elementary Grades*.

How can you build on students' strengths and provide for their success? Sometimes it means modifying the techniques you use as a teacher to meet student needs. Read what the same male student teacher wrote the following week:

> We were finishing up assessments for this marking period and my lessons included activities related to this. We did the telephone game on *sol, la,* and *mi* patterns and almost every kid was successful with it once I used my falsetto voice and not my real singing voice. We were luckily able to retest some kids who did not do so well the first time and they nailed every pitch the second time when they heard my higher vocal model.

SUMMARY

> I am really excited about how far I have come in my teaching of primary students; I am able to give directions clearly now in a quick manner so I can always keep music going in the classroom. My sequencing has gotten much better and I am actually having fun while I teach the kids; it has now become hard to just sit and observe as I really just want to teach.

General music teachers have a unique opportunity to impact the lives of every child in an elementary school. Sadly, for many children, their experience in fifth-grade general music may be one of their last exposures to a broad range of music if they are not part of a middle school performing group later. General music provides a foundation experience for future, hopefully *lifelong,* music learning.

SAMPLE LESSONS FOR ELEMENTARY GENERAL MUSIC

SAMPLE LESSON PLAN

MELODY
SINGING (So-Mi)
Grades K–2

National Standard: 1, 3

Concept: Music can have a melody consisting of only two pitches.

Objective: Students will sing a So-Mi song, using body movements and hand signals.

continued

Materials:
: "One, Two, Tie My Shoe" (Traditional)
  "Rain, Rain" (Traditional)

Sequence:

Give instruction: "Be my echo."

1. Sing "Yoo-hoo" on So and Mi, respectively.

2. Ask students how many different pitches there were (2). Which one was higher, "Yoo" or "hoo"? ("Yoo.")

3. Tell students that we can show that one pitch is higher and one is lower by using our bodies. Are the two sounds very far apart? (No.) Then our movements will need to be fairly close together, too.

4. Introduce the students to two pitches using Body Scale; chest for So (5), and hips for Mi (3).

5. Sing the song, using the body movements to indicate So and Mi.

6. Repeat, substituting "5" and "3" for the words to song, or "So" and "Mi."

7. Transfer body movements to Curwen hand signals for "So" and "Mi."

Questions:

How many pitches did this song have? (2)
How did we show the way the melody went back and forth between the two pitches? (body movements or Body Scale, hand signals)
What two special syllables/words do we use for these two pitches? (So and Mi)

Evaluation/Assessment:

Listen for pitch accuracy. Watch for students who need help with body movements/hand signals. Assess which students can do "all of the time," "some of the time," or "not yet."

Extension:

Add resonator bells for So and Mi. Have students "sound out" tune. Use "So-Mi" to turn poems into songs (Jack Be Nimble, Hickory Dickory Dock, or any others). Teacher or students lead.
Add "La" as used in "Rain, Rain."

Creativity:

Have students create their own So-Mi (or So-Mi-La) songs by leading the class in a Follow the Leader game, or, having "Puppet Conversations."

SAMPLE LESSON PLAN

BEAT
MOVING, LISTENING
Grades 3–6

National Standard: 6

Concept: Music can have a steady beat. Latin American pop music can have a distinctive style.

Objective: Students will use body motions to the beat.

Materials: recording of "La Bamba," by Los Lobos and an unpitched Latin American instrument (maraca, guiro, claves, etc.)

Sequence: Have the class sit in a circle.

Give instruction: "Think of an action you will do to the beat for this 'mystery song' – something we could all do after seeing it just one time. Everyone will get a turn to be the leader. This is the speed . . . It's fairly fast, isn't it? (Demonstrate speed by clapping with a 2-finger clap, inviting the class to join in.) Once we start, I'll use this instrument sound to signal that it's the next person's turn. Show me that you are ready with the action you will lead the class in by standing up." Class is in a standing circle.

1. When ready, start the music. After the introduction, the student immediately on your left demonstrates his beat-action; everyone joins in.

2. After each long phrase/section (usually sixteen or twenty-four beats), use the instrument to "signal" that it's the next person's turn to lead the class. Give everyone a turn to lead as you go around the circle. *Adjust the amount of time with each to best fit the music's form.*

3. When the music is nearly over, the speed of the beat *changes.* See if the class can adjust to the new speed.

4. Rewind the tape and repeat if all students did not get a turn to lead.

One possible translation:

> *In order to do the bamba (to dance La Bamba),*
> *it is necessary to have a little ability.*
> *A little ability for me, for you, and upward, and upward.*

continued

and upward, and upward for you I will be,
for you I will be, for you I will be.
I am not a sailor, I am not a sailor,
I am a captain, I am a captain, I am a captain.

Questions: When did the speed of the music change? (near the end) Was it faster or slower than the speed of the beat we were keeping? (slower) Who knows the special term we use for "the speed of the beat"? (tempo)

Evaluation: Check for beat competency.

Extension: Use a different recording of "La Bamba" or another song such as "Oye Mi Canto" by Gloria Estefan and the Miami Sound Machine, or any other favorite Latin American pop music. Compare this style with that of other popular Latin American music performers such as Celia Cruz, Ruben Blades, or Tito Puente, or to *mariachi, jarocho,* or Andean music.

SAMPLE LESSON PLAN

LISTENING, PLAYING, CREATING
HARMONY, FORM
Grades 5–8

National Standard: 2, 4, 6

"Blues for TJ" by B. B. King and Larry Carlton
[Blues in C]
Recording Used: *Guitar Fire!* (Gold Encore Series), 1993
GRP Records Inc., 555 W. 57th St., NY, NY 10017
Also Available on: *Larry Carlton and Friends*, MCAD-42214, GRP

Step 1—**Prepare, Listen, and Identify**
Listen to the recording while following along with the progression. Allow students to figure out the missing bass notes/chords.

C	C	C	C
?	?	C	C
?	?	C	C

(Answer in "Creative Activity" section of this Lesson Plan.)

continued

Step 2—**Participate**

Learn the added bass notes/chords and play with the recording. Play 12-bar blues bass note/chord progression in whole notes on xylos, metallophones, or melody bells. If desired, add borduns (5th above bass) or entire chord.

Step 3—**Question and Discuss**

- How many times is the 12-bar progression heard? (per segment played)
- Are there any differences in the repetitions of the progression? Describe the differences.

Step 4—**Listen Again**

Focus on the above questions. Play along, adding rhythmic improvisation, changing borduns (5th-6th-5th), entire chords (triads), or unpitched percussion such as a "ride" cymbal pattern.

Step 5—**Followup**

Listen to other 12-bar blues pieces (for example, *Ain't Nothin' But a Hound Dog* by Elvis Presley) and compare the type of bass used (walking bass, boogie bass, etc.). Explore the numerous styles that can be used with the same progression.

Creative Activity/Extension/Evaluation

In groups of 3 or 4, create a 12-bar blues piece with one student playing the bass on bass xylo or metallophone (if available), one chording or improvising on other xylos, metallophone, or melody bells (if available). Add a rhythm instrument to keep the beat. Practice several versions then perform for the class. Add lyrics in the following form:

Form for lyrics:

a	⇨	C	C	C	C
a′	⇨	F	F	C	C
b	⇨	G	F	C	C

Example: *Woke up this mornin' and found myself feelin' oh, so blue,*
I said, I woke up this mornin' and found myself feelin' oh, so blue,
When I went to leave the house, couldn't even find a matching shoe.

If desired, present the beginning of the first line to guide students: "Woke up this mornin' and ..."

*Note: Composed lyrics can be performed simultaneously **with** recording.*

Have students tape record their compositions and evaluate their group work with specific criteria.

Guided listening lesson format adapted from Sandra Stauffer (in Campbell and Scott-Kassner, 2002).

QUESTIONS FOR DISCUSSION

1. Recall your elementary school music experiences. What is your strongest memory of those years? What opportunities did you have to be engaged actively in music? How did these experiences influence your later music experiences?
2. General music is in danger of being cut back or even eliminated from the curriculum in many school districts. How would you "make a case" for keeping general music in the schools if you were speaking to a school board?

ACTIVITIES AND ASSIGNMENTS

1. Observe and participate in an elementary general music class. What types of activities were the children engaged in? Did music learning take place? How do you know?
2. Interview an elementary general music teacher. What are the challenges and rewards of teaching this age group?
3. Look at computer software such as *Making Music* or *Making More Music* by Morton Subotnick, *Music Ace I* or *Music Ace II*, *Band in a Box*, or software correlated to current basal series music textbooks for elementary school. How might these be utilized effectively in a classroom?

REFERENCES

ANDERSON, W. and LAWRENCE, J. (2001). *Integrating Music into the Elementary Classroom* (fifth ed.). Belmont, CA: Wadsworth/Thomson Learning.

BRUNER, J. (1966). *Toward a Theory of Instruction.* Cambridge, MA: Harvard University Press.

CAMPBELL, P. and SCOTT-KASSNER, C. (2002). *Music in Childhood: From Preschool through the Elementary Grades* (second edition). Belmont, CA: Wadsworth Group/Thomson Learning.

GARDNER, H. (1983). *Frames of Mind: A Theory of Multiple Intelligences.* New York: Basic Books.

KAPLAN, P. and STAUFFER, S. (eds.). (1994). *Cooperative Learning in Music.* Reston, VA: MENC.

Music Educators National Conference (MENC). (1994). *National Standards for Arts Education.* Reston, VA: MENC.

PIAGET, J. (1952). *The Psychology of Intelligence.* Trans. Percy, M. and Berlyne, D. E. London: Routledge and Kegan Paul.

Silver Burdett: *Making Music.* (2002). Parsippany, NJ: Scott Foresman/Pearson Education.

STAUFFER, S. (Ed.). (1995). *Toward Tomorrow: New Visions for General Music.* Reston, VA: MENC.

The Music Connection. (1995). Morristown, NJ: Silver Burdett Ginn.

The Music Connection. (2000). Parsippany, NJ: Silver Burdett Ginn/Scott Foresman.

Valuable Internet Resources

American Orff-Schulwerk Association <http://www.aosa.org>

Dalcroze Society of America <http://www.dalcrozeusa.org>

McGraw-Hill School Publishing Company <http://www.mhschool.com>

Music Educators National Conference; MENC also has a Society for General Music <http://www.menc.org>

Organization of America Kodály Educators <http://www.oake.org>

Silver Burdett Ginn/Scott Foresman Publishing Company <http://www. sbgmusic.com>

Look at & write short something about.

5

General Music in the Secondary School

Alexandra was eager to observe the teaching responsibilities of the choral director, Mr. Novak, at Northview High School. She arrived early in the morning, since Mr. Novak's chamber choir began its rehearsal at 7:30 A.M. After this rehearsal, he had two other choir rehearsals—women's chorus and the concert choir. After lunch, Mr. Novak told Alexandra that they had arrived at the point of the day when his "other life" began; his next classes were middle school general music classes.

Alexandra was quite surprised. "Have you been trained to teach these classes? Why would the choral director have to do this?"

"It's just part of the job. I do the best I can, but no, I was not prepared much during my undergraduate years to teach nonperformance classes. Never did I imagine teaching such courses. My sights were set on conducting choirs at the high school level. I have learned a lot by 'doing' and teaching the classes. My students also seem to learn best by 'doing' music—listening, composing, analyzing, evaluating, singing, playing instruments—instead of reading about music or listening to me lecture."

This brief, yet honest, conversation with Mr. Novak shed light on the music appreciation class that Alexandra was to observe. The bell rang. The class consisted of some students who appeared genuinely interested in being in the class. For others, it was clear that being in music class was not their priority.

The class was hardly what Alexandra had encountered in her middle school experience. The activities she observed did not parallel her expectation of teacher lecture and the students taking notes or copying musical vocabulary terms from the chalkboard. In fact, Mr. Novak seemed to incorporate consciously many musical behaviors and activities suggested by the *National Standards for Arts Education*. Alexandra's favorite moment of the class was when the class experienced improvisation, playing on melody bells and Orff instruments. Having studied the blues for the past few class sessions, the students sang a blues tune. They reviewed the progression of the twelve-bar blues. Then . . . Mr. Novak asked the class to improvise using the blues progression. Alexandra had noted some mild resistance from some of the students in the class—resistance that she had fully anticipated. But the students sang, some played notes belonging to chords of the blues progression in a steady beat on the melody bells, some students improvised a rhythm or melody on the Orff instruments using the notes of a specific chord when it occurred in the progression. Mr. Novak even showed three students how to play the primary chords on the guitar—one student playing a chord on a guitar. Later, the students created their own blues verse in

small groups and accompanied themselves while improvising on the "standard" blues progression. Such a sight to see the students smiling, participating, and making music! For Alexandra, this was a sure sign of a musically engaged class!

INTRODUCTION

In the scenario above, we experienced a frequent employment situation—a conductor of performance ensembles (instrumental or choral) who is also required to teach general music classes as part of her/his teaching responsibilities within a school district. Perusing college catalogs, it is apparent that choral methods, string pedagogy, and instrumental methods courses are readily available for music education majors while only a few institutions offer courses in the content and the pedagogical skill needed to teach general music-type classes in the secondary schools. In this chapter, we will raise philosophical, pedagogical, and curricular issues surrounding this paradox called general music education in the secondary schools.

SECONDARY SCHOOLS

Music Educators National Conference (MENC), the national professional organization to which thousands of music educators belong, held the following as its slogan: "Music for every child, every child for music." Implicit in this statement is that every student, regardless of age, has the right to receive music education throughout her/his school years (K–12). Although music education in elementary schools is common in many areas, it is rare to find diverse music opportunities throughout secondary school education.

Secondary schools have various grade-level configurations, but the most common grades included are Grades 6–12. Before middle schools were created, junior high schools of Grades 7–9 existed. They were literally referred to as "junior" high schools, since they were "mini" high schools. That is, students' daily class schedules resembled that of high school students' academic schedules. In addition, students were typically grouped according to ability level, creating homogenous classroom settings.

In the 1980s, middle school configurations became the educational trend. School administrators viewed Grades 6–8 as a necessary transitional period. Students adjusted from elementary schools, when they stayed with a "homeroom" teacher and class for the entire day, to high schools, when they changed classes and teachers throughout the school day. Middle schools, therefore, consist of students who stay together for "core" subjects with a team of "core teachers." Students also choose electives—heterogeneous classes such as music, visual arts, physical education, languages, and so on. Theoretically, middle school students should have the opportunity to explore many curricular domains and elective courses before they attend high school.

ADOLESCENTS

Who are the students in the secondary schools? Assuming a typical journey throughout secondary school, students ages 12–14 attend middle school, while students ages 15–18 attend high school. During middle school, the most radical changes are noted among our music students. Middle school years include sometimes drastic and unpredictable emotional, social, physical, and intellectual transitions for our students.

Shull and Vende Berg (Hinckley, 1995, p. 13) noted the following contradictions as they observed middle school students engaged in the struggle to leave childhood and to enter adulthood.

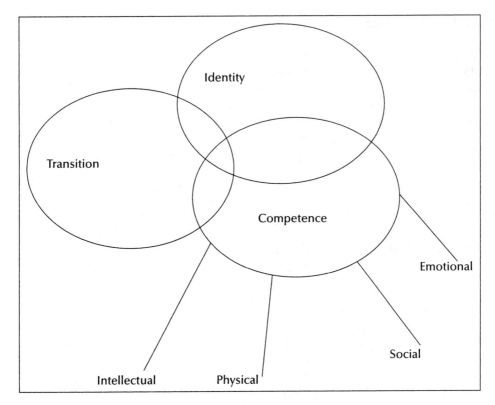

FIGURE 5.1. ADOLESCENT YEARS (AGES 12–18)

Contrasting Behaviors of Adolescents

Wishes to be independent	Very dependent on peer group
Struggles for freedom	Yearns for structure, especially from adults
Has adult vocabulary and knowledge	Uses childlike logic and feelings for making decisions
Has a short attention span	Can obsess on a subject of interest
Anxious to wear adult clothing	Embarrassed by growth into adult body
Exhibits high energy level	Submits to lethargy and depression
Displays an air of confidence	Feels insecure about self and relationship with peers
Denies affection and approval of adults	Seeks affection and approval of adults
Can seem like an adult in a child's body	Can seem like a child in an adult's body

What do some music education majors who are developing methods and skills necessary to teach adolescents *expect* to see as they observe adolescents in a middle school general music class? Many of the behavioral and emotional qualities that appear on their list are stereotypical descriptions of adolescents. Here are some collegiate students' expectations of adolescents *prior* to working with adolescents:

- wanting to be "cool"
- being unfocused/not on task
- being silly and immature
- having physical differences (height) within and between genders
- being "softer" than high school students—more willing to try different musical experiences
- having changing voices
- possessing raging hormones
- being talkative
- showing enthusiasm
- exhibiting childlike chubby faces and yet trying to act like adults
- being trendy, involved in distinct social (peer) groups
- fidgeting
- not wanting to be "singled out" for positive or negative reasons by the teacher
- asking random questions
- having a desire (at some level) to please the teacher
- being reluctant to perform "solo" activities
- slouching
- looking for outlets of self-expression, but only in private

After working with adolescents for one semester, the collegiate students had to revise their lists of stereotypical descriptions. In fact, they found working with adolescents in a music setting to be a rather positive experience! Most of the adolescent students eagerly tried new activities in music class, willingly provided and justified responses to teacher questions, and exhibited a great deal of energy for small group work and project-based instruction. They were an inquisitive group of students!

Given the apparent developmental and personality dichotomies evident during the middle school years, teaching music to these students can be full of joy, rewards, challenges, and frustration. A music teacher can walk into her/his classroom on one day and the students will be cooperative and attentive. The next day, the same teacher can meet with the same music class in exactly the opposite atmosphere. Moods, attitudes, and relationships are constantly in flux. Students are highly critical of themselves, are very self-conscious of appearing incompetent in front of their peers, and are often tormented by what they perceive their peers *think* of them. Their perceptions versus their realities sometimes do not coincide.

Students look at teachers as authorities whose word and direction they will challenge with their own adolescent "logic." By contrast, they look to teachers to provide and maintain high musical expectations and freedom for creativity within a classroom structure. Many teachers fall into the trap of attempting to be secondary students' "best friend." This leads to difficulty, for the teacher's task is to be friendly and courteous, but yet to be the adult facilitator of music education.

By the time students arrive in high school, many of the difficult transitions that occurred during middle school ease in intensity. Students are fast approaching adulthood. Developmentally, students have reached what Piaget termed the "formal operations stage" of development, a period in which students and adults develop the mental ability to make decisions and formulate arguments based on concrete logic, rather than a mix of emotion and illogical conclusions. As students' attention spans increase, independence is key, and students become focused on career goals and their future lives.

SECONDARY SCHOOL MUSIC OPPORTUNITIES

There are two basic genres of music education programs in secondary schools—performance (band, orchestra, chorus) and nonperformance (general music, music theory, technology, composition, music appreciation). Each program exists to fulfill specific, yet not disparate, music education functions. Performance opportunities will be discussed in separate chapters of this book. The general music program serves to expose students to a variety of musical experiences, styles, and genres, while building foundational music "literacy."

Recently, there has been a professional debate as to whether music classes in the secondary schools should be labeled "general music" or "nonperformance" classes. Perhaps these terms are misnomers, since the *National Standards for Arts Education* (MENC, 1994) call for both performance and general music classes to contain experiences that include performance and nonperformance musical opportunities. That is, performance opportunities such as singing, playing, composing, and improvising are to be included in the general music classes, along with opportunities for describing, listening, analyzing, and learning cultural and historical contexts of world musics. After all, to understand music is to "know" it in many situations that include creation, organization, and perception of musical sound.

A strong music education curriculum (K–12) would ensure that the secondary school music curriculum would be an extension of the comprehensive music curriculum implemented at the elementary school level. Therefore, basic musical concepts—harmony, rhythm, duration, pitch, form, tone color, dynamics—first introduced in the elementary school grades would be revisited at a more sophisticated level of teacher presentation and student engagement at the secondary school level. This "spiral curriculum" idea should still incorporate the same musical behaviors (singing, playing, composing, listening, improvising, moving) that students experienced in elementary school, except that the secondary school students would be asked to exhibit these behaviors to a higher degree of proficiency and music conceptual understanding. New musical terminology can also be attached to students' own descriptions of the music they experience or create in class. Music concepts to be experienced cross the boundaries of grade level, while the activities students experience are variable and need to be designed as "age-appropriate" learning opportunities.

While the content of middle school general music classes tends to consist of a broad survey of musics and musical experiences, Hinckley (1995, p. 136) suggests that high school general music courses should delve deeply into musical issues according to the students' interests and cultural community. In addition, she urges high school general music classes to provide students ample opportunities to pursue independent music projects according to individual students' musical skill and interests that are relevant to their lives. Perhaps students and the music teacher could determine together the musical journey they will take during the course of a general music-type class.

What type of general music course electives might exist at the high school level? Related arts (combined and integrated content of music, visual arts, literature, dance, theater, and other artistic domains), electronic music, music theory, music appreciation, recorder, guitar, composition, multimedia/music technology, music criticism, and world musics are only a few of the possibilities that could be offered to high school students. These general music classes might attract those students whose music education might not otherwise be served because they do not participate in performance ensembles or because they do not have the financial resources to rent instruments or to study privately. Therefore, general music classes have the potential to strip the notion of elitism from music education.

Students in some locations are typically required to take one quarter or trimester of general music during their middle school years. After sixth grade, however, students who wish to be in band, orchestra, or chorus seldom continue to participate in general music classes. It is important to note that graduation requirements vary per state.

Music teachers often face middle school students who appear unmotivated to be in music class, who have signed up for class simply to fill their schedules, or who were placed in the class by administrators or school counselors. All is not hopeless! Given a creative music educator, these students can become motivated and meaningfully involved in music learning. The key is to start at the "place," the base of knowledge and experience, from which the students are coming to your music class. As Maxine Greene states, "Surely, at least part of the challenge is to refuse artificial separation of the school from the surrounding environment" (1995, p. 11). Using music with which students are familiar, the music educator can make connections from their concrete music experience to the more abstract and newer musics that the students have yet to experience. Musical bridges are built that minimize the differences between "real music" and "school music."

The use of technology as a tool for teaching and learning can be a hook in creating music "elective" courses at the middle or high school levels. Students might learn to compose at computer stations, complete with synthesizers, sequencers, and music software. Software exists that supports computer assisted instruction; it serves as a tutorial for music students. That is, students can work individually or with a partner to develop a particular musical skill (i.e., music theory and aural skill development). Some software is an interactive exploration (on a CD-ROM) of a specific piece of music or of a particular historical period of music. Additional software is available for notation, sequencing, and developing student creativity. Secondary school students might experience a composition course as a music elective, and students might learn to arrange music for a choir or band. Students in the secondary-school general music class who have not had private instrumental or vocal training might find a synthesizer to be a wonderful means of composing without having to know how to play the piano. Piano keyboards (using electronic keyboards) are available in some schools to give students the opportunity to learn basic keyboard skills.

Students who enroll in general music classes at the high school level are most likely to be those who choose not to participate in ensembles. Unfortunately, most states require only one fine arts requirement for graduation, a requirement that may or may not be fulfilled by students who opt to take a music course in high school. Consequently, many high school students have not experienced music instruction since their middle school years.

GOALS OF GENERAL MUSIC IN THE SECONDARY SCHOOL

The goals of general music education at the secondary-school level should parallel those stated for any grade level of a child's music education. As teachers, we strive to awaken the imagination in a way that is unique to music and art. We seek to raise adolescents' curiosity and interest in music, so that they will become lifelong consumers and active participants in musical activity. We recognize that music and the arts are means for keeping our culture alive. We look to build informed audience members. We aim to develop

independent musical thinkers. We strive to facilitate the development of our students' human sensitivity, their musical perception, and their appreciation of the art of musical performance and its creative process.

A REFLECTION: A FIRST TEACHING EXPERIENCE IN A MIDDLE SCHOOL GENERAL MUSIC CLASS

After her first teaching experience in a middle school general music classroom, one student provided the following reflective commentary about her teaching.

Lesson on Early Radio, Jazz

In general, I think this was an effective lesson. I think the students responded well to the subject matter and me; they were attentive and engaged in the activities. I was going to do a bit more with my lesson plan by comparing jazz of the Twenties and Thirties to contemporary jazz types, but I realized that the lyrics on the album I wanted to play as modern jazz were not appropriate. I followed what the class gave me more than my lesson plan. The idea of syncopation was brought up, so we went with that for a few minutes, and followed the rhythmic patterns of the style. I believe my goals were still met, the students realized that they were identifying a "jazzy feel" in terms of rhythm and timbre, but I think my closure could have been more specific. I did see almost all of them keeping the steady beat, and they did all attempt to move to it, and even tried the Charleston!

Responses were not all bad, there were several quiet students, but for the most part the class answered my questions. When I asked each of them to respond with what instruments they heard they actually did, which was nice. There were the usual unsolicited responses.

Noteworthy Moments

Pedagogy: missed opportunity: occurred when the term "syncopation" was brought up and it was not explained fully. One of the students defined it as "off beat rhythms" and I left it at that. It was a good opportunity to take what they had given me and help them understand it.

Climate: effective action: occurred when I encouraged the students, and they all attempted to dance. It was clear that they felt comfortable enough to try something a little silly and embarrassing.

Musical thinking/performing: effective action: occurred when I followed up on answers students gave me to my question of what they heard on the beats. I kept asking them to think and listen closely, and also move so they would feel the music and the beat.

Classroom management: effective action: occurred when I asked the students to stand. They were all getting pretty slumped in their seats and a little antsy at the same time, so I had them move on their feet.

Another Glimpse from Another Student

Here is another observation of a collaborative process between a collegiate music methods student and his professor of music education. Together, they were planning for an upcoming middle school general music lesson. Compare the manner in which this description is different from or is similar to the preceding descriptive reflection. Which is evaluative in nature? Are student outcomes addressed in the descriptions? If so, to what degree? Which appeals to you as the reader? Why? How might the format of one and the style of another description be merged? How would the reflective description read?

Preparation for the Tuesday middle school general music lab in the public schools was underway. In the office sat the professor with her secondary music methods student. Together, they had decided to focus on a comparative listening lesson that would involve a review of the movement experience from the "Sunrise" (Strauss, *Also Sprach Zarathustra*) lesson presented last week and "Sunrise" from Grofé's *Grand Canyon Suite*. The methods student's task was to create a movement sequence for the latter piece and then to compare both listening examples.

"I know the students cooperated with you last week, but you're the teacher! If I try to do this movement, they will not do it. I just know how adolescents are! Plus, I'm a guy. They're going to laugh at me!" The professor responded, "When we are in the classroom, we are both the music teachers. You must maintain a high expectation that every student will participate. If they know your expectation and you make the task interesting and accessible, I bet they will cooperate." The methods student reluctantly agreed to take on the task of creating a movement sequence, admitting that he, himself, felt uncomfortable with the idea of moving his body to music.

Tuesday afternoon arrived. The methods student was dressed very professionally and was obviously quite nervous. The middle school general music students entered the class. The professor reviewed the Strauss "Sunrise" by having all the students "echo" the movement sequence while listening. So far, so good. Most of the students were engaged.

Then it was time for the methods student's lesson segment. At first, his countenance appeared quite stern. He had his lesson plan thoroughly prepared. He asked questions, he was sequential, and it was clear that he expected all to participate. During the movement and listening activity, it was evident that he realized that he had created a captivated audience among the middle school students. A broad smile crept across his face. At the completion of the movement sequence, he resumed his role of methods student, looked at the professor, and exclaimed, "Wow! This really *can* work!" Comparative discussion between teacher and his music students ensued.

LESSON PLAN

Grade: 6

Lesson Content: Conclusion of brass family unit

Goal: Tone color of brass instruments

Prior Knowledge: brass instrument unit

Materials: Chalkboard, stereo system, large pictures of instruments, recording of Strauss's *Also Sprach Zarathustra* and Williams's "Theme from *Star Wars*"; listening handout

Objectives: Students will be able

- to identify tone colors of the brass family.
- to sing and identify Do, Sol, Do as played by a brass instrument.
- to perform a movement sequence while listening to a piece of music featuring brass instruments

Procedure:

1. Listen to the theme from *Star Wars*.

   Q: When in the movie is the music heard?

   Q: What kind of a mood is established by the music?

   Q: Does the mood stay the same?

2. As students listen again to *Star Wars*, have them circle descriptors on handout.

3. Discuss descriptors and why students responded as they did.

4. Play another recorded mood-setting piece of music from a movie that uses brass instruments: "Sunrise" from *Also Sprach Zarathustra*.

5. Have students sing and hand sign Do, Sol, Do.

6. Listen to *Also Sprach Zarathustra* and have students raise hand each time they hear Do, Sol, Do.

7. Identify which instrument plays Do, Sol, Do each time.

8. Perform a movement sequence (students echo movements performed by teacher). Discuss how the music is reflected in the movements.

What follows is a sample handout for students.

Listening Guide for "Theme from *Star Wars*"

Circle the words that describe what you hear as you listen to the musical excerpt.

Column A	*Column B*
Energetic	Relaxed
Adventurous	Easygoing
Gently rhythmic	Strongly rhythmic
No beat	Strong beat
Loud	Soft
Mostly strings and woodwinds	Mostly brass
Melody move by leaps	Melody move by step (scales)

Other words to describe what you are hearing:

MOVEMENT SEQUENCE R. STRAUSS: "SUNRISE" FROM *ALSO SPRACH ZARATHUSTRA*

Repeat this sequence three times, each time making motions larger to indicate growing intensity:

- Begin in a crouch position; fingers tapping on the floor
- Curwen hand signs (Do, Sol, Do), gradually standing
- (Cymbals): Arms explode upward
- (Timpani): Feet jog and then march

After third repetition, continue with:

- Right arm curve, left arm curve
- (Trumpet): hands move upward following melodic contour
- (Trombone): Arms extended at side and descend; add timpani part by jogging/marching
- Circle arms twice
- (Cymbals): jump; large, complete body shake
- Small, complete body shake (subito piano)
- (Crescendo): growing large, complete body shake
- (Organ): Stand, smooth hand line crossing in front of body

DISCUSSION OF LESSON PLAN

1. Why is it important for music educators to stipulate learning outcomes/ objectives for each lesson?
2. Describe the nature of the teacher's questions.
3. Which activities are performance-oriented? Nonperformance-oriented?
4. Which *National Standards for Arts Education* are included in the lesson plan?
5. How would a middle school general music teacher recognize whether student learning had occurred during the lesson?
6. What classroom management issues might arise during these lesson plans?
7. How does the lesson plan progress from concrete to abstract (from familiar to unknown) for the student?

QUESTIONS FOR DISCUSSION

1. Recall your secondary school music experience. What opportunities did you have to be engaged actively in music? How did these experiences influence your decision to explore music education as a possible career choice?

2. Should all secondary school students, even those in performance ensembles, be required to take general music classes? Why or why not?

3. If you were able to design the music requirements for a secondary school, what music instruction would you require? For how many years? semesters? quarters?

4. What "nonperformance"(general music) electives would you include at the high school level? Explain your choices.

FOLLOWUP ACTIVITIES

1. Provide examples of contemporary or world musics familiar to adolescents that you might use in a general music classroom in order to provide a bridge to their tolerance and understanding of other genres of music (i.e., "classical" music, jazz, electronic).

2. Contact several middle schools and high schools. Survey the types of music performance opportunities that are offered to their students. What are the state requirements for music instruction at the secondary school level?

3. Observe a middle school general music class. Record what you see and hear. Note the differences between genders, level of class involvement, and variety of musical activity.

4. Interview a secondary school general music teacher. What other teaching responsibilities might she/he have? What are the challenges and rewards of teaching general music at the secondary school level?

REFERENCES

Books and Articles

GREENE, M. (1995). *Releasing the Imagination*. San Francisco: Jossey-Bass.

HINCKLEY, J. (1995). "Issues in High School General Music." In Stauffer, S. (ed.), *Toward Tomorrow: New Visions for General Music*. Reston, VA: MENC.

Music Educators National Conference (MENC). (1994). *National Standards for Arts Education*. (1994). Reston, VA: MENC.

SHULL, S. and VENDE BERG, K. (1994). "The middle school learner." In Hinckley, J. (ed.), *Building Strong Programs: Music at the Middle Level*. Reston, VA: MENC.

Valuable Resources

FOWLER, C. (1994). *Music! Its Role and Importance in Our Lives*. Mission Hills, CA: Glencoe/ Macmillan.

HOFFER, C. (2001). *Teaching Secondary Music* (fifth ed.). Belmont, CA: Wadsworth.

REGELSKI, T. (1981). *Teaching General Music: Action Learning for Middle and Secondary Schools*. New York: Schirmer.

REIMER, B. (ed.). (2000). *Performing with Understanding: The Challenge of the National Standards for Music Education*. Reston, VA: MENC.

THOMPSON, K. and KIESTER, G. (1997). *Strategies for Teaching High School General Music*. Reston, VA: MENC.

Valuable Internet Resources

American Music Conference
<http:www.amc-music.com>

American Orff-*Schulwerk* Association
<http://www.aosa.org>

Association for Technology in Music Instruction
<http://www.music.org/atmi>

National Coalition for Music Education
<http://www.amc-music.com>

Professional Associations

International Society for Music Education (ISME)
International Office
P.O. Box 909
Medlands 6909, WA
Australia
++61-(0)8-9386-2654
<http://www.isme.org>

Music Educators National Conference (MENC)
The National Association for Music Education
1806 Robert Fulton Drive
Reston, VA 20191
800-336-3768
<http://www.menc.org>

Organization of American Kodály Educators (OAKE)
1612-29th Avenue South
Moorehead, MN 56560
(218)227-OAKE (6253)
<http://www.oake.org>

Society of General Music (SGM)
(see MENC website: <http:www.menc.org>)

6

Band Programs
and Performances

Both the director and students were becoming extremely frustrated because nothing was going right in rehearsal. The spring concert was two weeks away and although the band had been working on the music the past two months, progress was slow because the music was too difficult. According to the director, the band couldn't play the correct rhythms, phrase, play in tune, or do the correct articulations. The frustration pushed the director to shout angrily to the students: "What is the matter with you! I explained the correct rhythms to you yesterday. Can't you remember to do anything right?"

The director then fell into the trap of beating time on the music stand with the baton and resorted to rote teaching. After rehearsal, many of the best students went to the principal and complained that the director was being unreasonable and they wanted to quit band. The next day the principal had a conference with the director and made the suggestion to stop shouting and start teaching.

That night, the director went home depressed and thought about looking for another job. Once home, however, and relaxed, the director started to think about what the principal had said. That evening, the director began to write down creative techniques that would motivate and inspire the students, and looked forward to tomorrow's rehearsal.

How was the rehearsal scenario reminiscent of your rehearsal experiences in high school band? Discuss effective rehearsal techniques and contrast them to ineffective techniques in this scenario. Was the frustration in the rehearsal because of the director's teaching techniques, the music, or the students' preparation, or the upcoming concert? What aspects of preparing for concerts are rewarding or frustrating?

In this chapter, we will examine the history of bands in America, including professional bands, community bands, and the phenomena of the rapid growth of the school band movement indigenous to the United States. We also will present practical suggestions to raise the musical standards of band performance in preparation for concerts and contests. And, finally, we will discuss ways in which a director may improve rehearsal techniques by understanding the relationships between music and the other arts.

BAND HISTORY IN AMERICA

Information on early bands in America is somewhat sketchy, but one of the earliest bandmasters was Josiah Flagg (1737–95), who organized and directed the first regular militia band of Boston. He presented a concert with the Boston Militia Band on June 29, 1769, with fifty musicians in the ensemble. Flagg formed his own band in 1773 and gave a few concerts, but "secular music was not encouraged in New England, and it is probable that Flagg's career as a bandmaster was short-lived" (Goldman, 1961, p. 34).

Our first great American bandmaster was Patrick S. Gilmore (1829–1892), who generally is regarded as the father of the concert band in the United States. He came to the United Sates from Ireland in 1848 and settled in Massachusetts, where he became leader of several bands before organizing his own in 1859. As an outstanding conductor and cornet virtuoso, he changed the history of the concert band in America. As he enlarged the concert band repertoire with his excellent transcriptions, he also raised the standards of band performances. Gilmore's band of sixty-six musicians received recognition throughout the United States and Canada and also in Europe in 1878 with outstanding concerts that were well received each place that he visited. John Philip Sousa stated that Gilmore's band was "equipped to a greater degree of musical perfection and artistic merit than any known organization of that day" (Chase, 1966, p. 624). Gilmore, also known under the pseudonym of Louis Lambert, wrote the famous Civil War song "When Johnny Comes Marching Home," which was published in 1863.

The most popular bandmaster that ever lived was John Philip Sousa (1854–1932). His popularity was due to the following factors:

1. He became internationally renowned because he gave the public music it wanted to hear—he believed that the function of the band was for entertainment and not education.
2. He was a musical genius who composed marches that had tremendous appeal to audiences throughout the world. Marches at that time also were used for ballroom dances as well as parades. Sousa's artistic description of a march was "it must be as free from padding as a marble statue. Every line must be carved with unerring skill. Once padded, it ceases to be a march" (Hitchcock, 1974, p. 120).
3. He was the first bandmaster to make use of radio and recordings, thus reaching a larger audience than anyone before.
4. The period in which his band flourished was from 1880 to 1925, which was perfect for professional bands, because there was no competition from orchestras and therefore bands were the only source for popular entertainment.

5. And, finally, when Sousa formed his own professional band in 1892, he entirely changed the normal instrumentation of the band by decreasing the number of brass and percussion instruments and increasing the number of woodwinds. He also introduced a harp.

The virtuoso musicians in Sousa's bands were capable of performing programs on the level of those of any professional symphony orchestra. According to Goldman (1961), the size of Sousa's band varied according to the repertoire and circumstances. Normally, it had an instrumentation of sixty-five players, but at its largest, it numbered about seventy-five.

The best-known professional band conductor after Sousa was Edwin Franko Goldman (1878–1956), also a prolific composer of marches and a great force in American band music. The personnel of his band was chosen from the best professional musicians in New York and is still active today.

Another professional band active today is the Detroit Concert Band, under the direction of Leonard B. Smith, whose recordings of band classics titled "Gems of the Concert Band," originally released between 1978 and 1989, are now on five compact discs and are outstanding examples of band performances.

Robert Boudreau, born 1925, founded the American Wind Symphony, which specialized in the performance of contemporary wind music and commissioned works for band.

Military bands in the United States are also excellent examples of professional concert bands. The United States Marine Band is the oldest, founded in 1798, is now conducted by Lieutenant Colonel Timothy W. Foley. The establishment of other military bands includes: The Navy Band (1918), the U.S. Army Band (1921), Air Force Band (1942), and Army Field Band (1946).

COMMUNITY BANDS

A movement parallel to the professional bands in early America was the development of the town community bands. The oldest community band still performing today was formed in Allentown, Pennsylvania, in 1828; it is second in longevity only to the Marine Band. The band was so good that John Philip Sousa recruited Allentown band members to play in his ensemble. Outstanding guest conductors over the years have included a "who's who" of prominent bandmasters: Edwin F. Goldman, Herbert L. Clarke, Henry Fillmore, Arthur Pryor, Paul Lavalle, Lucien Cailliet, Leonard B. Smith, Donald Voorhees, William Santleman, Keith Brion, and Frederick Fennell.

Participation in a community band serves as a valuable experience for adult musicians who wish to continue their music education. Community band is also the ideal performance ensemble for area music teachers, and it provides the director added visibility and credibility as a leader in the community. But most of all, there is that inner aesthetic satisfaction of seeing musicians of all ages working to perform outstanding music together.

SCHOOL BANDS

While the college bands throughout America were run by students to provide entertainment for sports events, especially football, college bands did not really develop until Albert Austin Harding (1880–1958) was appointed acting student leader of the University of Illinois Band. He was so successful that he was later considered the father of college band directors; he was the first person to succeed in raising college bands to a symphonic level, and he is credited with 147 band transcriptions. John Philip Sousa so admired Harding that he left his entire music library to the University of Illinois.

Under Harding's leadership, the fame of the University of Illinois bands spread throughout America and influenced other colleges and universities to establish outstanding band programs. According to Frederick Fennell, "The concert bands of the University of Wisconsin, Northwestern University, Ithaca College, the Symphony Bands of Oberlin College, University of Michigan, and the Eastman School Symphony Band are but a few of the many large and magnificently instrumental organizations that have come into existence since A. A. Harding began his work at Illinois in 1905" (Fennell, 1954, p. 49).

The growth of school bands is truly an American phenomenon based on the following contributing factors (Prescott-Chidester, 1938, pp. 3–10) :

- Bands served as entertainment at athletic competitions.
- Excellent high school programs started by A. R. McAllister in Joliet, Illinois (1912), that served as an outstanding model for other schools throughout the nation.
- Students began receiving credit for instrumental music, for meeting after school in Richmond, Indiana (1905), and for taking private lessons after school in Chelsea, Massachusetts (1905). Charles McKay gained both school time and credit for instrumetal music in Parsons, Kansas (1920).
- The first national band contest, sponsored as a promotional device by instrumental manufacturers, was held in Chicago in 1923. Manufacturers turned management of future contests over to school boards. The first school-sponsored national contest was held in 1926 in Fostoria, Ohio, with 315 bands in the competition. The contest was won by the Fostoria High School Band under the direction of John Wainwright, who later gained wide attention for his pioneering work in music education. The rapid growth of bands in America can be attributed to music contests. By 1932, over one thousand school bands were competing in national contests.
- Joseph Edgar Maddy (1891–1966), the first supervisor of instrumental music in the schools of Rochester, New York, was a pioneer in the development of instrumental music. He established the National Music Camp at Interlochen, Michigan, to supplement the regular instruction of the school year.
- A. A. Harding and Edwin Franko Goldman organized the American Bandmaster Association in New York City in 1929 and encouraged composers such as Henry Cowell, Gustav Holst, and Percy Grainger to compose for band.
- William D. Revelli became director of bands at the University of Michigan in 1935 after developing championship high school bands at Hobart, Indiana, that won five consecutive national championships. Revelli became a major influence in the band movement as an outstanding interpreter of band literature and had extremely high performance standards. He founded the College Band Directors National Association, which has been a major influence in establishing performance standards. Revelli continued in the tradition of A. A. Harding and became the dean of American band conductors.
- The next major change in band history was at the Eastman School of Music, when Frederick Fennell announced the formation of the Eastman Wind Ensemble in 1952. Under Fennell's conducting genius and the virtuosity of the

Eastman players, the ensemble became known to band directors throughout America through a series of recordings and compact discs.

- Finally, as we look back over two hundred years of band history in America, we can say instrumental music has made phenomenal progress.
- School bands are stronger than ever, as the institutions of higher learning continue to produce music teachers of outstanding ability and dedication. This progress will continue as long as the future band directors dedicate themselves to the musical advancement of bands through the medium of American education.

MARCHING BAND

The high school marching band will be recognized as a positive force in music education if it is approached with the same high standards as the other ensembles found in a comprehensive music program. The role of the music teacher in the public schools is to teach music. If the band director maintains high standards of musicianship with the marching band and teaches the band to play musically with proper attention to tone quality, intonation, phrasing, correct embouchure, dynamics, subdivision, and style, then these concepts will carry over to the concert band.

The problem with many marching bands is that they forget that they are a musical organization first and a marching unit second. When this happens, marching bands are criticized for too much emphasis on volume and distorting embouchure. The organizations we produce as music teachers reveal us as entertainers or educators. As long as the director keeps the marching band balanced, musical, and in proper perspective with the other school ensembles, it can be an important part of the total music program and an educational experience for the students.

The marching band is often the first musical organization the general public will see, and they may judge the quality of the entire music department based on the quality of the half-time show. While this may be unfortunate, it is a realistic expectation that the public would like to see a quality marching band at the football game. The director should realize the importance of a marching band based on solid music fundamentals in selling the complete marching program to the school and community.

JAZZ BAND

Jazz is part of our American heritage. As a truly indigenous art form, jazz has made a unique contribution to music history. Students benefit from a variety of experiences by performing in jazz band. Participation in jazz band is educational because it exposes the student to a variety of musical styles, techniques, and articulations not commonly found in concert band. But, most important of all, it allows the student to be creative through the study of improvisation. The study of improvisation is one of the many reasons for having this type of organization available to students. To be able to understand jazz harmony so that a student can compose and perform a solo simultaneously in rhythm is indispensable for total musical growth.

Additional reasons for offering jazz band as a component of the school curriculum are that it teaches:

- musical confidence by having responsibility of one to a part
- exposure to advanced rhythmic challenges
- flexibility and sight reading by exposure to different jazz styles
- spontaneity through improvisation
- expanded technical ranges and expressive possibilities for all instruments

Suggested Listening

Charlie Parker	John Coltrane	Dave Brubeck Quartet
Duke Ellington	Count Basie	Mel Lewis
Modern Jazz Quartet	Thad Jones	Woody Herman

BRITISH BRASS BAND

One successful import from the United Kingdom that is quickly experiencing a rebirth of interest in America is the British style brass band. Indeed, with over forty thousand brass bands in Great Britain alone, the recognition of the brass band movement in America is rapidly growing. After the first North American British Brass Band Championships were held in Raleigh, North Carolina, in 1983, their visibility has increased throughout America. One reason for their popularity is the unique sound of the band because of their homogeneous brass band instrumentation, which creates a warm dark timbre that is pleasant to hear. Instrumentation consists of soprano cornets, flugel horns, tenor horns, baritones, Euphonium, trombone, and basses. Except for the bass trombone, all instruments read from the treble clef and have identical finger patterns. Publishers now, however, print bass clef parts for first and second trombones and basses on the reverse side of treble clef parts in order to make the music more accessible to American bands. Composers and arrangers of the brass band repertoire are the noted English composers Gustav Holst, Edward Elgar, Malcolm Arnold, Gordon Jacob, Dennis Wright, Philip Sparke, John Ireland, and Edward Gregson. Outstanding examples of British brass bands performing their repertoire can be found on CDs released by the Black Dyke Mills Band and Besses O' th' Brass Band.

WHY REPERTOIRE MATTERS

Teaching is essentially the act of believing in students, of hoping that we have given them the inspiration to dream big dreams, to stretch their imaginations, to connect them to that wonderful world inside themselves, which they should not waste or forget as they go on in life. As many students struggle to find a place in this world, music teachers will continue to give them an emotional anchor through the performance of worthwhile music.

The chief aim and responsibility of a music teacher is to choose well-crafted literature of high quality that will develop the musicality of students and stimulate their emotional growth as well. What students will remember years after their ensemble experience is not how many trophies were won, not the contests, nor the trips, but the music they performed. If we played music that flounders in a morass of mediocrity, then we have produced mediocre students. However, if we performed music that throbs with the splendor, pain, and beauty of life, students will be inspired to develop a passion for the arts. Emotions are the shortest distance between two planes of understanding. When people hear music that reflects humanity, they may find meaning and purpose when all else seems hopeless. Substantial music reflects the magnificence of the mind and spirit of mankind.

BAND REPERTOIRE

As a future music teacher, your choice of music for performance will reflect your philosophy, values, aesthetics, and performance standards. Select compositions that will fit the band. The primary purpose of a musical performance is to express, not to impress. Choose a work of substance with technical demands that do not surpass the group's ability to play expressively. Literature of substance is easy to teach because it is spiritually uplifting. Easy, formulaic pieces will become boring both to you and the students after a short time (Knight, 1986).

Choose music to challenge the best students; their interest and enthusiasm for the piece will motivate the other players. Select at least one slow, expressive work, because this will give the band opportunities to improve in basic tone quality, breath support, intonation, balance, and interpretation. Finally, choose music that you like.

The compositions of the following composers are good examples of suitable and substantial music recommended for high school bands.

Malcolm Arnold arr. Paynter	Four Scottish Dances
	Prelude, Siciliano and Rondo

Leslie Bassett	Designs, Images and Textures
Robert Russell Bennett	Suite of Old Americans Dances
Elliot Del Borgo	Do Not Go Gentle Into That Good Night
Leonard Bernstein arr. Beeler	Overture to Candide
John Barnes Chance	Incantation and Dance
	Variations on a Korean Folk Song
Aaron Copland	An Outdoor Overture
	Variation on a Shaker Melody
Norman Dello Joio	Scenes from the Louvre
Vittoria Gianinini	Fantasia for Band
Morton Gould	Ballad for Band
Percy Grainger	Irish Tune and Shepherd's Hey
	Lincolnshire Posy
Edward Gregson	Festivo
Howard Hanson	Chorale and Alleluia
	Laude
Walter Hartley	Sinfonia No. 4
Gustav Holst	Suite No. 1 in E flat
	Suite No. 2 in F
Karel Husa	Al Fresco
Charles Ives	Variations on America
Gordon Jacob	William Byrd Suite
William Latham	Three Chorale Preludes
Francis McBeth	Kaddish
	Of Sailors and Whales
Darrius Milhaud	Suite Francaise
Ron Nelson	Rocky Point Holiday
Vaclav Nelhybel	Symphonic Movement
Vincent Persichetti	Pageant
	Divertimento for Band
	Symphony No. 6
Alfred Reed	Russian Christmas Music
	Armenian Dances 1 & 2
H. Owen Reed	La Fiesta Mexicana
William Schuman	Chester
	George Washington Bridge
Gunther Schuller	Meditation
Fisher Tull	Sketches on a Tudor Psalm
Clifton Williams	Symphonic Suite
	Fanfare and Allegro
Ralph Vaughan Williams	English Folk Song Suite
	Toccata Marziale

MUSIC PERFORMANCE AND THE MUSIC CONTENT STANDARDS

In a performance-based curriculum, the rehearsal focus is on eliminating errors in preparing for the next concert. The problem with this philosophy is that it usually depends too much on rote teaching of skills without comprehensive understanding to prepare students for future musical growth. A typical rote rehearsal would emphasize the technical aspects of performance and include: finger technique, imitation, repetition, precision, and articulation, providing for a performance that is routine but not necessarily musical.

When teachers move beyond the technical trenches and teach with comprehension, some wonderful musical growth starts to happen. Through the creative teaching of the intrinsic concepts of music such as melody, rhythm, harmony, form, texture, and mood linked with the music content standards, a teacher is able to take students to a deeper level of understanding, teaching students musical insights that will last a lifetime.

INCORPORATING THE MUSIC CONTENT STANDARDS IN A REHEARSAL

In *Turning Notes into Music*, Hans Lampl warns music teachers to avoid the Procrustean approach to performances, because is does not allow for musical freedom and flexibility (1996, p. 130). Procrustes was an evil giant in Greek mythology who forced his victims to lie on a bed too short for them and then cut off any overlapping body parts. If the bed was too long he would stretch his victims to fit its length.

The Procrustean approach is used far too often in a rehearsal that places the major focus on technical rather than musical understanding. For a performance to have depth of interpretation, both the conductor and musicians must be feeling the music together. Incorporating the music content standards in a rehearsal will help achieve this depth of feeling and produce a rehearsal atmosphere that is built on trust and understanding.

Standard No. 1: "Singing alone and with others a varied repertoire of music"

Desultory warmups on the same B♭ major scale every day can be musically harmful; it can lull your students to sleep and perhaps you as well. Warming up on a Bach chorale by singing and playing is a creative way to increase your students' attentiveness. Have the brass play the first phrase of a chorale and have the woodwinds sing the second phrase on a "la" in response. Next have the woodwinds play the next phrase, and the brass sing the fourth phrase in response and so on throughout the chorale. To foster inner hearing, have the band play the first chord of a chorale together, then silently sing their parts to a certain point at which the conductor gives a downbeat to come back in singing to check their pitch. Stopping every so often at cadential points and having different sections sing the chord and identify its color (major, minor, augmented, diminished) is a good practice. Singing in an instrumental rehearsal is one of the best ways to teach phrasing and intonation. Singing automatically erases the barlines, which gives the music a certain spontaneity and freedom that is often lacking in instrumental performances. Use the vocal approach to emphasize the point of maximum tension in the climax of a phrase and then relate it to instrumental playing. By giving lyrics to an instrumental composition, phrase attacks and releases will be much smoother and the phrase will have direction.

Standard No. 2: "Performing on instruments, alone and with others, a varied repertoire of music"

In a performance-based curriculum, this standard will be covered through the use of solos and ensembles. However, more emphasis needs to be placed on performing a varied repertoire throughout the year. Directors should not forget that the late Renaissance and early Baroque periods are rich in musical substance. A comprehensive music program should include music from all periods and styles from the Renaissance to twentieth-century minimalist.

Standard No. 3: "Improvising melodies, variations and accompaniments"

The jazz band satisfies this standard completely because students are expected to improvise original melodies over given chord progressions. This has been a deficiency of concert band training in the past, but now directors have taken lessons from their jazz counterparts and are writing out chord progressions and having students warm up over different chordal patterns. Moreover, the following composers have written works that require students to improvise:

Barnes, James. "Invocation and Toccata." Publisher: Southern
Paulsen, John. "Epinicion." Publisher: Kjos
Peck, Russel. "Cave." Publisher: Galaxy Music
Pennington, John. "Apollo." Publisher: Schirmer

Standard No. 4: "Composing and arranging music within specified guidelines"

What better place to teach the elements of compositional techniques than in a rehearsal? Most students love to arrange compositions for small ensembles and bands. One of the major faults in a performance-based curriculum is that the director is so occupied with the next performance that fundamentals are not taught. Teaching the elements of theory, arranging, and composition in a rehearsal will help students to learn the music in rehearsal much faster.

Standard No 5: "Reading and notating music"

Students should be able to use both standard and nonstandard notation to record their musical ideas and the musical ideas of others. In a concert band setting, there has always been a major deficiency between what students actually hear and what they can play on their instruments. Because of the emphasis on psychomotor techniques and not comprehension, musicianship is sadly lacking. To remedy this problem, the director could use creative ear-training techniques in the rehearsal. The director could use the piano to dictate intervals and melodic lines from the music in rehearsal and have students write them down and then play it back on their instruments to check for accuracy.

Standard No. 6: "Listening to, analyzing, and describing music"

This standard can be accomplished by listening to a recording of different style periods such as Baroque, jazz, classical, and blues, then asking students specific questions that will guide their listening for deeper understanding. Perhaps the most important part of a musical experience in a rehearsal is the art of concentrated listening when we take in everything around us so that our individual parts fit into the whole. Too often, in a band rehearsal, the listening is too passive without focus. To teach active listening, band directors can take their cue from general music teachers who provide musical road maps that include history, music vocabulary, flow charts, and instrumental color to keep their students interested. A simple question from the band director such as "What do you hear and feel in the music?" will heighten students' awareness to deeper musical meaning and understanding. The objective of focused listening is to reveal something new in the composition each time you listen.

Standard No. 7: "Evaluating Music and Music Performances"

Students will improve in behavior and musicality in direct proportion to the models they evaluate and imitate. It is the responsibility of the director to provide exemplary models to raise students' standards of excellence. Only by listening to the best recordings and playing music of substance will students have an appreciation of the importance of music in their lives.

Standard No. 8: "Understanding relationships between music, the other arts, and disciplines outside the arts"

Developing the skill and knowledge base necessary to include this music content standard in a band curriculum is also essential for the artistic growth of a music educator. Searching and studying music outside of our usual spheres may stimulate new thinking. The emotions within a Beethoven symphony may add to our understanding of music by Percy Grainger. Knowledge of

Verdi operas may add drama and lyricism to our interpretations of other works. Listening to string quartets may add a chamber music quality to a large ensemble.

Good directors never accept the status quo, but continue to develop their intellectual and artistic perspective. Directors should look to the arts and see the relationships between great literature, dance, art, drama, and conducting music.

To learn instrumental color and mood, study the paintings of Van Gogh. If you want a baton technique that has both economy of motion and substance, analyze the prose of Hemingway. To teach an ensemble to understand rhythm, review the teachings of Emile Jaques-Dalcroze. Directors who want to add pacing and drama to rehearsals should study the works of Shakespeare and Eugene O'Neill. As these insights are applied to conducting skills, always share a love for music with students. Remember what Beethoven wrote on the score of his *Missa Solemnis*: "From the heart—May it go to the heart."

Standard No. 9: "Understanding music in relation to history and culture"

The final standard, understanding music in relation to history and culture, is probably the most important of all. If we can make an effort to understand the music of different people, then we can understand their history and behavior because music is a reflection of society. We can teach acceptance and respect when we remember that inside each society there is a diversity of many types of music representing, among other things, distinctions in age, race, and religion.

BAND LESSON PLAN

Grade Level: Middle School Band

Musical Concepts: Motivic development and thematic transformation, musical pitch, instrumental color, dynamics and articulation

III. Music Content Standards:

No. 1 Singing, No. 2 Performing on instruments, No. 6 Listening to, analyzing, and describing music, No. 7 evaluating music and musical performance, No. 8 Understanding relationships between music, the other arts, and discipline outside the arts

continued

IV. Objectives: Students will be able to . . .

- Sing major themes of Nelhybel's *Festivo*
- Circle each time the minor third motive occurs
- Listen to a CD of *Festivo* and make evaluations
- Understand the conducting patterns for espressive, legato, marcato, and staccato
- Correct use of the tongue for various dynamics
- Understand musical time relevant to musical interpretation
- Understand the importance of instrumental color

V. Procedures

1. Teacher will have the students listen to a CD of *Festivo* in order to understand the style of *Festivo* and how their part fits into the composition.

2. The melody of the composition is based on an ascending two-note motive of a minor third and its subsequent thematic transformation. The teacher will have students sing and recognize minor thirds and find examples in their music.

3. To teach the concept that each musical tone, no matter how short, should have pitch, sonority, and resonance, the students might sing the first pitch of *Festivo* using a *tah* syllable while fingering the note on their instrument.

4. In measure 61, the woodwinds enter at the same volume level as the brass for excellent antiphonal effect. Record the ensemble at this point and discuss the relationships between music and other art forms, pointing out how Nelhybel paints his music with different instrumental colors. As an assignment, students might create pictures that look like Nelhybel's music.

5. The teacher could demonstrate the different styles of the composition by using the analogy of arms moving underwater for espressive legato and for staccato the flick of the baton much like a finger bouncing off a hot stove.

6. At measure 160, the woodwinds often distort the articulation by playing the FF dynamic with too much tongue. The solution to this problem is to have the students blow the air FF but tongue PP for less movement of the tongue.

VI. Lesson evaluation: To determine if *Festivo* is ready for performance, the conductor will give the first downbeat, stop conducting, and step off the podium. The band will play through the complete composition while the teacher walks around the room listening for rhythmic drive, dynamic contrast, clear releases, and precise tempo changes that capture the spirit of the composition.

ASSIGNMENTS

1. Write a paragraph describing the difference between a performance-based curriculum and a comprehensive curriculum and how each effects musical growth.
2. How would you incorporate the music content standards in an instrumental rehearsal?
3. Our involvement in music is due to outstanding role models that have made a positive influence in our lives. Please describe in one paragraph the circumstances of your own personal history, of how you got started in music.
4. What were the contributing factors that can be attributed to the rapid growth of school bands in America?
5. Discuss band compositions that have made a substantial impression on your growth as a musician.
6. The primary purpose of a band in an educational setting is to educate students. Discuss ways a music teacher can keep music contests and performances in perspective for her/his students.
7. Discuss the relationships between great literature, dance, art, drama, and teaching music.

REFERENCES

Books and Articles

CHASE, GILBERT. (1966). *America's Music* (rev. second ed.). New York: McGraw-Hill.

FENNELL, F. (1954). *Time and the Winds*. Kenosha, WI: G. Leblanc.

GOLDMAN, R. (1961). *The Wind Band*. Boston: Allyn and Bacon.

HITCHCOCK, H. W. (1974). *Music in the United States: A Historical Introduction* (second ed.). Englewood Cliffs, NJ: Prentice Hall.

KNIGHT, J. (December 1986). "Bach and the Band Director." *The Instrumentalist Magazine*, 41, pp. 46–51.

KNIGHT, J. (January 1989). "Contests: Agony or Ecstasy?" *The Instrumentalist Magazine*, 43, pp. 13–18.

KNIGHT, J. (April 1998). "Lessons from Hemingway." *The Instrumentalist Magazine*, 52, p. 47.

KNIGHT, J. (May 1999). "Indelible Moments." *The Instrumentalist Magazine*, 53, p. 2.

LAMPL, H. (1996). *Turning Notes into Music*. Lanham, MD: Scarecrow Press.

PRESCOTT, G. and CHIDESTER, LAWRENCE. (1938). *Getting Results with School Bands*. Chicago: Carl Fisher.

Valuable Resources

American Bandmasters Association
1521 Pickard
Norman, OK 73072-6316
405-321-3373

American School Band Directors Association
P.O. Box 146
Otsego, MI 49078-0146
616-694-2092

Association of Concert Bands
2533 S. Maple #102
Tempe, AZ 85282-3559
800-726-8720

Conductors' Guild, Inc.
103 High St., Room 6
West Chester, PA 19382-3262
610-430-6010

The Instrumentalist Magazine
200 Northfield Road
Northfield, IL 60093
847-446-5000

International Association of Jazz Educators
P.O. Box 724
Manhattan, KS 66505-0724
913-776-8744

National Band Association
P.O. Box 121292
Nashville, TN 37212-1292
615-343-4775

Women Band Directors National Association
P.O. Box 63
Murfreesboro, TN 37133-0063
615-898-2993

Pygraphics—Pyware
P.O. Box 639
Grapevine, TX 76099-0639
800-222-7536

7

String Education

It was a few days before the winter break and the beginning string class was re-viewing tunes for their concert. The school had a festive atmosphere and one of the students asked if the group could play "Jingle Bells" for their classroom and teacher. Ms. Green, the string teacher, thought about it for a minute and sug-gested, "How about strolling through the halls and serenading the whole school?" The students thought it was a great idea. Ms. Green said she would need to check with the principal and if it was approved they could stroll during the time of the next string class. The cellists said, "How are we going to walk and play since we need to sit down to play?" Ms. Green suggested they think about solutions to that and be prepared at the next class.

The principal approved and Ms. Green notified the string students. She checked with the cellists and they discovered they could walk with the cello by

wrapping their fathers' belts through their pant loops and around the ribs of the cello. The day arrived and the students were so excited to share their music. Ms. Green tuned their instruments and led the parade with a hand drum to keep the tempo steady. Off they went around the school playing "Jingle Bells" with the greatest of gusto! That was one event not soon forgotten for those students.

String and orchestra teaching is imbedded in the "old world" of European musical tradition. Although the instruments themselves—violin, viola, cello, and bass—have evolved over many years, our finest examples were made by Stradivarius and Guarnerius in Italy in the 1600s. One of the first pieces of music to incorporate a complete orchestral instrumentation was the opera *Orfeo*, composed by Claudio Monteverdi. String players enjoy a wealth of music from composers such as Vivaldi, Mozart, Copland, and Corigliano. Traditionally, orchestra has been viewed as a challenging discipline, in which a great many alternative styles of music exist that involve stringed instruments broadening the image of string performance.

DEVELOPMENT OF STRING CLASSES

Professional orchestras have existed in the United States since the New York Philharmonic was founded in 1842. At the end of the nineteenth century, the first school orchestras grew out of a desire to have the traditional music of the "old country" here in America. After World War I, more players were needed for the orchestras, and attention was turned to developing musicians in the schools.

Boston had been the site of the first singing schools, but group instrumental teaching was unknown at this point. There were a few scattered early school ensembles with an interesting combination of whatever instruments were available—a violin, a trumpet, a trombone, perhaps a string bass. Instruments were expensive as they were made primarily in Europe. These instruments were often found in attics and were formerly played by relatives who probably brought them from Europe. The teacher usually taught this group one by one and then arranged classical pieces for the performers to play together.

By the 1900s, music was an established part of school. On hearing about a class string method in England, the music supervisor of Boston sent Albert Mitchell to study this program in Maidstone outside of London. Mr. Mitchell saw a gymnasium full of students playing violins together well. He eagerly learned about their process of instruction and on returning to Boston wrote the Mitchell Method in 1911.

From this modest beginning, others heard about the method and were eager to adopt it. New ensembles formed in the Midwest under leaders such as Joseph Maddy, Frank Laycock, and Paul Herfurth. These men also were key in bringing the need for academic credit for high school players to the attention of a national meeting of principals in Dallas in 1927. An honor orchestra of students from many different programs was gathered to perform for this meeting. From these roots, the National Music Camp was developed by Joseph Maddy and Thaddeus Giddings and founded at Interlochen, Michigan.

Competition has always been a strong motivator for students and teachers. In 1932, the national orchestra competitions began and served as a forum for ensembles to share in their excitement of high quality music-making.

Today's Public School String Class

String classes today are most frequently found in suburbs of larger cities. Typically, students begin instruction in fifth grade and meet once or twice a week. Students usually are "pulled out" of an academic class to go to string class, a practice that presents difficulties for some. The teacher travels between several elementary buildings and often teaches a junior high or high school orchestra as well. Space for string class is often inadequate and difficult to find. Some classes combine violin, viola, cello, and sometimes bass together. Dedication is what keeps string teachers dealing with these less-than-ideal teaching settings.

Usually, the secondary strings programs are part of the daily school schedule and share a rehearsal room with the band. These ensembles often progress rapidly and can attain high levels of performance standards. Uniforms and motivational events such as trips and competitions are expected with these groups.

Solo and ensemble competitions also encourage teachers to offer chamber music in some string programs. Even though chamber music ensembles enhance students' independence and general musicianship, they are more difficult to schedule and therefore are less frequent.

Private lessons do much to allow for individual development. Private study primarily occurs at the student's own initiative, but some districts allow lessons in the schools, enabling more students to benefit from this assistance.

Although orchestra programs have tended to flourish predominately in the larger cities, smaller cities also have successful string instruction if there is a dynamic teacher. Financial civic support is perenially affected by economics and often results in the elimination of some strings programs. Recently, however, research has supported the rich benefits available from music instruction, and growth of orchestra programs has resulted.

OTHER ORCHESTRAL OPPORTUNITIES

Community Youth Orchestras

Community youth orchestras are ensembles composed of students from a broad geographic region who audition and then rehearse weekly throughout the school year. These groups are often associated with a school district or professional symphony orchestra but can be independent. Tuition is ordinarily involved, but scholarships are often available. Students who seek to participate in youth orchestras are leaders in their school groups and have dedicated and supportive parents who enable them to participate in additional ensembles. Most students in these ensembles also take private lessons. Some upper level groups include college-age players. For the younger orchestras, it is possible that a college student might assist in coaching youth orchestra sections for experience.

Honor Orchestras

Music educators' associations in each state organize regional and state honor ensembles. Where there are string programs, there are honor orchestras. Honor ensembles offer a special, exciting experience for students to play with other dedicated young musicians.

Summer Camps

Many summer camp opportunities for string players also offer opportunities for young people planning to teach, as counselors or teaching assistants. Camps are a stimulating opportunity for students to perform with other motivated string players.

Chamber Ensembles

Chamber ensembles are an enriching addition to any string program. More and more repertoire is being published for young chamber ensembles. After a chamber ensemble has prepared their music, they can begin to perform in the community for a variety of functions. Community performance by student groups are a wonderful public relations tool for the music program.

Fiddlers or Strolling Strings

Many programs have discovered the advantages of forming a small ensemble of students to perform for informal public functions to highlight the benefits of string instruction. Fiddling is a popular form of string performance. It is one of the oldest musical genres in America, and came from Europe with the early European immigrants. The recent resurgence of Irish dancing and other folk dancing provides a natural venue for fiddlers to perform. Music is readily available and accessible for young fiddle players. Andy Dabcewski and Bob Phillips (1999) have provided some collections of tunes for young string players of a mixed instrument class structure. There are also collections by Red McCloud for strolling string groups to play in the style of gypsies. These groups are extremely mobile—they actually walk around and do not require chairs or music stands because the music is usually memorized. Students in the group are coached on the importance of visual interaction with the audience, so the result is a highly stimulating performance.

Preparatory Programs

Many institutions of higher education offer preparatory music programs as outreach opportunities for teaching by their faculty or students. The American String Teachers Association with the National School Orchestra Association has supported preparatory programs, describing the University of Texas at Austin String Project as a model. String players begin in the elementary school and continue through the highest level offered. Students in the program typically participate in private lessons, group theory, and an ensemble.

STRING PEDAGOGUES

Paul Rolland

The school string method books did not change substantially over the twentieth century, although the authors were influenced by innovative string pedagogues. One of these pedagogues was Paul Rolland (1910–79), founder of the American String Teachers Association, who came to America from Hungary with his string quartet. He first taught violin at Simpson College in Iowa and realized that the old way of teaching resulted in very stiff posture. He then moved to the University of Illinois at Champaign-Urbana, where he researched and developed a sequence of motions that would enable players to have more flexibility in their playing. Literature that resulted from his work includes *The Teaching of Action in String Playing* (1974), *Prelude to String Playing* (1971), *New Tunes for Strings* (1971) by Stanley Fletcher, and a series of short films to demonstrate his ideas. Students in the films were young students from the central Illinois area that he taught to demonstrate his ideas. The films, produced in 1968, although a bit dated, are still pertinent and informative to students and teachers.

Flexibility and balance, based on studying kinesiology and dancers' movements, are the hallmarks of Rolland's approach. The films include demonstrations of golf swings and baseball pitches that are compared to similar movements in string playing. Preparation for movements and balance in the body are the focus. Freely moving exercises such as shuttling up and down the fingerboard develop a relaxed instrument hold and are a precursor to shifting. The films and the book *Teaching of Action in String Playing* include many additional exercises that are helpful in all levels of string playing. Principles generating from Rolland can be found in method books published in the latter part of the twentieth century.

Shinichi Suzuki

A major influence for string teaching in the twentieth century was Shinichi Suzuki (1900–99). His book, *Nurtured by Love* (1969), describes his pedagogical journey. Suzuki was the son of a Japanese instrument manufacturer and, after studying violin in Germany, returned to Japan and formed a quartet with his brothers. After the collapse of financial markets in 1929, he supplemented his income by teaching children to play violin. During World War II, his violin work was suspended. After the war, he started a music school in Matsumoto, Japan, where he developed a sequence of repertoire that is careful and thorough in technical progress. The material is taught in private lessons with tunes played by groups of students on the same instrument. Study begins with "Twinkle, Twinkle Little Star" in variations. These variations are derived from rhythm patterns in the Baroque music literature. The majority of pieces in the first book are folk tunes, selected so that one new playing technique is added at a time. There are ten books, concluding with the Mozart Violin Concerto in D Major.

Suzuki's teaching is based on a strong foundation of philosophy that believes in nurturing the student in a positive environment. A tremendous aspect of his contribution to teaching is this philosophy. Instead of teaching through intimidation and force, the student should be guided and motivated to play by the teacher and parent. Suzuki felt that if children could learn to speak a language at age three, then they could learn to play the violin as well. Because the students start this approach at such a young age, the use of demonstration is a key component but one that is a weakness if used exclusively. Parents are an integral part of the learning process for the child. This is often a challenge for today's busy parents. Over the years, teachers of this approach have included the instruction of theory and music reading along with the development of the ear through listening.

The Suzuki approach was first introduced to the United States at Oberlin College in 1958 by Clifford Cook, professor of string education, at a meeting of the Ohio String Teachers Association. A theology student from Japan

had presented Mr. Cook with a film of young students in Japan playing a festival concert. In the film, the gym floor had hundreds of students beautifully playing the Vivaldi A minor Concerto together. After viewing this performance, the approach was studied in Japan by these string teachers and brought to America for others to learn how to follow these ideas.

Because of the popularity of the Suzuki violin method, repertoire has been compiled for use by cello, piano, viola, flute, guitar, harp, and bass. Materials were prepared by teams of teachers with experience in using the approach with the violin. The Suzuki Association of America regulates the training of students and teachers in this approach through summer institutes and graduate programs at various universities across America.

Kato Havas and Phyllis Young

Other contributors to the changing view of string pedagogy have included Kato Havas (1920) and Phyllis Young (1926–). Ms. Havas, raised in Hungary, was impressed by the flexibility of gypsies as they played violin. After a concert career in Europe, Havas retired in England to raise a family. Havas believed that string playing should be executed in a flowing manner. She encouraged students to use imagery and singing to overcome physical playing obstacles. For example, she asked students to imagine they are playing their instruments and then to sing their parts as they moved their arms and bodies with the music in a pantomime of playing. Students then play the piece with their instrument and usually find the action easier. Her ideas were presented in *A New Approach to Violin Playing* (1961).

Phyllis Young grew up in Kansas, studied cello at the University of Texas at Austin, and then was selected to teach cello there. She was the first woman president of the American String Teachers Association and an active clinician in string pedagogy. Young used creative games to have students develop freedom in their playing, such as applying some imaginary ski wax on the left-hand fingers and then sliding them on the fingerboard between the strings and flying off the end like a ski jump. The purpose of this game is to align the fingers and arms with the instrument without forcing a proper position. Young's book, *Playing the String Game* (1978), is a very useful source that should be included in the teaching of string players.

Geza and Csaba Szilvay

The twentieth century closed with an approach similar to the beginning of string teaching in America, that of singing to assist learning to play a stringed instrument. Two brothers of Hungarian descent, Geza and Csaba Szilvay, who began their teaching in Finland, developed an approach based on the Kodály principles of music instruction. The approach includes singing using solfège, rhythm syllables, and composition to teach music literacy. The music is comprised of folk songs native to the students. The Szilvays' curriculum includes not only repertoire for preschool general music, violin, and cello beginning levels, and scale books but also commissioned music for beginning ensembles and string orchestra. Their early books use color to identify strings for the young players, a method called *Colourstrings* (1994). The Szilvay approach has produced many fine players who now occupy professional positions in the orchestral world.

LESSON PLAN FOR A STRING CLASS

Below is a sample lesson plan that might include some of the ideas proposed by these pedagogues. It is for any string player from second through fourth year of study.

Objective: To be able to play "Cotton-Eyed Joe" in an authentic style.

National Standards for Music: Listening and analyzing, notating, singing, improvising, performing, cultural history

continued

Prior Knowledge: holding of instrument and bow, playing the D scale

Materials: Tune sheet of "Cotton-Eyed Joe" in key of D in treble, alto and bass clef. An electric violin may be used for this music.

Procedure:

1. Listen to a recording of Appalachian Fiddling more than once, listening for repeated rhythm patterns. (listening)
2. Explain how this style derived from early settlers seeking entertainment and musical expression. (cultural history)
3. Identify and play open string rhythms that were found in the recording.
4. Have students write the rhythms on the board. (notate)
5. Sing the tune on the "Cotton-Eyed Joe" sheet. (singing)
6. Play the tune. (performing)
7. Improvise a rhythmic open string drone to accompany the tune.
8. Echo each students' rhythm pattern. (improvise)
9. Improvise additional rhythms to add to the tune.
10. Ask students to perform on melody or harmony together.

Assignment: Review variety of rhythms and freedom of the style of fiddling.

Evaluation: Assign another fiddling tune for students to prepare for the next class.

QUESTIONS FOR DISCUSSION OF THIS LESSON PLAN

1. What string pedagogues' influences are represented in this lesson?
2. How can this lesson be adapted for different levels of playing abilities for students?

EXPLANATION OF LESSON PLAN

A fiddle tune is a good core to a lesson because it offers many avenues of learning for the student. The entire class can learn the melody, not just the violins. Fiddle tunes can be taught aurally, which is traditional, or by reading the music notation. Ear-training can be involved in finding the harmonic drone and in echoing improvisations that are developed by each student. Initial improvisation is done in a cacophony of sound with all

students experimenting at the same time. Then they each perform their pattern, and the class echoes it, permitting each student to develop a repertoire of possibilities. During the step of adding rhythms to the melody, the teacher initially requests everyone to double one of the pitches every time it occurs. This step of the lesson not only involves knowing the note names but compressing a new rhythm into the framework of the tune. For the final performance students can be paired up in duets with one playing melody and the other playing harmony. These steps can then be applied to another tune.

Expectation of Levels

Beginning string players are comfortable in the keys of D, G, and later C major and e or a minor. These are the common keys in most Book I method books. The most accessible rhythms are quarter notes and eighth notes. The range of pitches in Book I tunes is within or close to an octave. A major goal for the first year is establishment of position and good tone production. Folk tunes are the basis of the repertoire in the method books. Arrangers that are successful for this level include Elliot Del Borgo, Mark Williams, Robert Frost, and John Higgins.

Intermediate string playing includes mastering the keys of F, B♭, and A major or d and g minor. Bowing variations become more complex with slurs and hooking of uneven rhythms. The range crosses the four strings of the instrument in the first position or without sliding the hand up the string. Vibrato and early shifting exercises are now common. Repertoire is more diverse with longer arrangements and compositions available including those by Merle Isaac, Sandra Dackow, Bill Hofeldt, Carold Nunez, and others. Some Baroque music is accessible in unabridged form.

Advanced string playing includes mastering all major and minor keys and being able to use a variety of bowing and style characteristics. Standard repertoire is accessible from the traditional and contemporary composers.

SKILLS NEEDED IN TEACHING

Because of a shortage of string teachers, American String Teachers Association with the National School Orchestra Association is seeking every avenue to encourage musicians to consider training and working as string teachers. String teaching at different levels of abilities requires different skills of the teacher. We have found that some very successful teachers are not major performers on stringed instruments but have gained a thorough knowledge of the sequences of teaching these instruments. Teaching the beginning stages of string playing requires demonstration, singing, and creative arranging skills, diagnosing and solving playing problems.

At the intermediate level, the teacher becomes more of a conductor. Much manual assistance in tuning and some position correction is still necessary at this level, so the teacher should not remain central on the podium the entire class time. Selection of repertoire is crucial to motivation of the ensemble. Music for intermediate players must be technically and musically appropriate, as well as sequenced in a manner to challenge yet be accessible for the players. The same qualities are important at the advanced level, and the inclusion of some of the standard orchestral repertoire is now possible for the players.

The most common public view of a string educator is that of a conductor. Although most music educators have a limited amount of time allotted to training as a conductor, summer schools and conferences are good places to improve these skills. Along with the necessary focus on gestures, teachers also should plan to continue to develop their musical skills. The most basic of these is ear-training, which is necessary for a conductor/teacher. The final element of a fine conductor/teacher is that of leader in the psychological sense. Groups need inspiration and goals in order to perform at their highest levels.

The string educator should guide the students to reach their highest playing potential and to perform with pleasing tone and pitch. It is important for teachers to keep abreast of current trends through music conferences and workshops that could benefit the students. It also is highly important for music teachers to continue to feed the fire that inspired them to enter the profession in the first place; that is best done by performing as a musician themselves. Some avenue of self-expression in music is necessary to stay motivated and to pass on this noble art.

SUGGESTED ASSIGNMENTS

1. Listen to Suzuki tapes and analyze the sequence of repertoire.
2. Watch videotapes on the Rolland approach.
3. Watch videotapes on the Havas approach.
4. Read and apply a Young string game with a young string player.

REFERENCES

Books and Articles

DABCZYNSKI, A. and PHILLIPS, B. (1999). *Fiddlers Philharmonic*. Van Nuys, CA: Alfred Publishing.

ERWIN, J. (1993). "Roots." *American String Teacher*, . 43(2), pp. 65–69.

FLETCHER, S. (1971). *New Tunes for Strings*. New York: Boosey and Hawkes.

HAVAS, Kato. (1961). *A New Approach to Violin Playing*. London: Bosworth.

PERKINS, M. (1995). *A Comparison of Violin Playing Techniques: Kato Havas, Paul Rolland, and Shinichi Suzuki*. Reston, VA: American String Teachers Association.

ROLLAND, P. (1971). *Prelude to String Playing*. New York: Boosey and Hawkes.

ROLLAND, P. (1974) *The Teaching of Action in String Playing*. Urbana: Illinois String Research Associates.

SUZUKI, S. (1969) *Nurtured by Love*. New York: Exposition Press.

SZILVAY, G. (1994) *Colourstrings*. Helsinki, Finland: Fazer Press.

YOUNG, P. (1978). *Playing the String Game*. Austin: University of Texas Press.

Professional Organizations

American String Teacher Association with the
National School Orchestra Association
4153 Chain Bridge Rd.
Fairfax, VA 22030
<http://www.astaweb.com>

Suzuki Association of America
P.O. Box 17310
Boulder, CO 80308
<http://www.suzukiassociation.org>

8

Choral Music Education

It is Thursday morning at Wilson High School. Approximately sixty-five high school students (Grades 9–12) gather for their daily choral rehearsal. This high school choir is comprised of students having a variety of previous choral experiences and singing abilities. As the singers become situated within their sections, a group of first-semester music education students also enter the choral rehearsal; their task is to observe the effectiveness of the interaction between the choral director and the singers.

The rehearsal began without the choral conductor having to say a word. She began the body stretching exercises, the singers stood, gradually became quiet, and followed the movements of the conductor. Next the conductor vocally demonstrated

a vocalise, which required the singers to maintain their intonation during a descending line. The singers performed this exercise and others without piano accompaniment. "Which of the five notes of the descending scale are consistently flat?" asked the conductor. "The second note. No, the third note," bantered the students. "Well, let's do it again, and this time listen to yourself and the others around you." The students sang again, and this time they noted that the third note was flat. The conductor suggested that as they sang the descending line, the students raise both of their arms above their heads. When they sing the lowest note of the descending scale, both arms should meet above their heads. "Okay, let's try it again with the movement." The students sang and incorporated the motion. A smile appeared on the conductor's face. "So what did you think of the way you sounded that time?" The choir responded, "It was more in tune." "Great! Let's try it once more, really concentrating, but without using the movement." Again, the choir responded by singing the descending line in tune.

"Before we begin rehearsing our literature, let's work a bit on exercise number seven on your sight-singing sheet." All of the students pulled the sheet from their folder. Although there are sight-singing books that can be purchased, the conductor often created rhythmic and melodic sight-singing exercises for her students. These exercises were based on challenging areas found within the literature that the students would eventually sing in concert performance. "Here's the tempo." The conductor conducted one measure of triple meter before the students sang the exercise using solfège syllables. After much struggle to find the notes of the fourth measure, the conductor asked the students to gather into small groups within their sections and to work out the notes and rhythms of that measure. Reconvening the entire choir after ninety seconds, the conductor gave another full measure of three beats, but this time the choir had mastered the sight-singing exercise. "As we rehearse this morning, I want to see who can tell me for which song this exercise was written. The tricky parts here, of course, were the last three intervals."

INTRODUCTION

Did you participate in choirs in the elementary, middle, or high school levels? What choral opportunities did you have from which to choose? What observations of this rehearsal do you think the first-semester music education students noted? What were some effective choral rehearsal strategies? What was similar/different when comparing this rehearsal to your own experience in choral rehearsals? What was the communication like between the director and students? Was the learning environment one of a shared learning partnership between students and teacher? How would you know from the scenario presented above? Included below is an excerpt from an observation report that was written by a freshman music education student. She noted that the choral rehearsal she had observed was quite different from her own secondary school choral experience. What qualities of the conductor, the students, or the rehearsal atmosphere might have contributed to an effective choral rehearsal?

> I walk into the building [where the choir rehearsed] and ask a kind security man where I could find the chorus. I didn't really even need to ask. This literally angelic sound came from upstairs in the building. I followed my ears; I was greeted with a wall of sound. I don't exaggerate! I was really impressed.
>
> The conductor, Ms. Lynn, stands on a podium so she can see every face and communicate to them as she conducts. She conducts with her **entire** body. Her arms make sweeps, her face alive and so in the moment that she looks as if she's ready to take flight from the podium. Ms. Lynn's energy reflected not only the music they were working on, but also being in front of a group of high school singers and for teaching. It looked as if she were in her glory. It just seemed her usual self, frequently smiling. A good sense of humor and yet an intensity for learning permeated the room.
>
> I was also really impressed with the way the conductor chose to do Vivaldi's *Gloria*. There was a large and varied repertoire that the choir worked on. I think it's wonderful when teachers use their resources to the fullest. If there's a violist or a horn player in your choir, put them to use somehow. Surely the singers do more than sing.
>
> I didn't see the conductor visibly show any signs of frustration or anger. She never snapped at a singer. It was really different for me because my teacher during middle and high school would tend to degrade us during our rehearsals. My choir reflected the attitude and lack of motivation that my teacher showed. In the choir that I was observing, [the singers] had such enthusiasm for what they were singing. They were also attentive. There was little talking while the conductor worked with other sections. The choir's sound was so pure, so blended, but they were not perfect either. But, Ms. Lynn and the singers explored ways of becoming the best musicians they could be. It was a pleasant and inspiring atmosphere to witness.

In this chapter, we will explore the historical perspectives of choral singing in America, the development of a comprehensive choral music education program that embraces music content standards, the development of the human vocal apparatus, and specific choral opportunities that exist in most public schools. A sample lesson plan specifically designed for a middle school choral rehearsal and discussion question concerning the lesson plan conclude the chapter.

HISTORICAL PERSPECTIVE

Vocal Music in the Early North American Settlements

Although Leif Ericsson and other Norsemen were the earliest Europeans to arrive in North America, their musical traditions brought from Europe remained only temporarily. The Norsemen danced and played pipes and drums. The native North Americans also had their rich cultural and musical

traditions. The two groups, with diverse cultural experiences, did not interact with nor participate in each other's musical traditions. Therefore, when the European colonizations disbanded, there was no vocal music tradition of the settlers' influence that remained with the native North Americans.

In spring 1564, three shiploads of Huguenots established settlements in what is now Jacksonville, Florida. They were Calvinists who were psalm singers. Native peoples of the areas surrounding their settlements came from far and wide to listen to this "foreign" singing. Unlike the Norsemen, the Calvinists encouraged the natives to participate by learning French psalm singing by rote. What were the Huguenots' motives for involving the native peoples in their singing?

British influence was evident by the landing of the Pilgrims at Plymouth Rock, bringing with them the *Ainsworth Psalter*. In 1640, the American rendition of this psalter was printed as *The Bay Psalm Book*, and it was recognized as the first book printed in America. There was a general mistrust of any music other than sacred music. Accounts of early worship services included these descriptions: (1) congregational singing was not a priority of worship services; (2) there was little part-singing in churches; and (3) people of the congregation knew only three or four songs to which they set their psalms.

Many of the new European settlers and the native North Americans were unable to read or write. How did the church pastors and deacons teach their congregations the psalm settings? "Lining out" a psalm seemed to be the most efficient way of teaching the psalms to the masses. Lining out was a method by which the pastor or layperson read or sang a phrase—a line of a psalm tune—and the congregation repeated it. Today, this method is still used with young children when teachers teach them a song by rote: the echo method. Here is an example of lining out the tune "Old Hundredth," taken from *The Bay Psalm Book*:

> Pastor: Make ye a joyful sounding noise.
> Congregation: Make ye a joyful sounding noise.
> Pastor: Unto Jehovah, all the earth;
> Congregation: Unto Jehovah, all the earth;
> Pastor: Serve ye Jehovah with gladness:
> Congregation: Serve ye Jehovah with gladness:
> Pastor: Before his presence come with mirth.
> Congregation: Before his presence come with mirth.

Singing Schools

During the 1720s, advocates of quality congregational singing challenged the lack of singing tradition in the church and founded singing schools to teach congregations to read music. They called for "regular singing" (singing by reading musical notes) rather than "old-style singing" (lining out melodies). In the Ninth Edition of *The Bay Psalm Book*, shaped notes were used, indicative of the "Fasola," or shaped note, tradition of reading music, different shaped notes related to different scale degrees. Later, John Tufts modified this method of reading and writing musical notation by placing initial letters of the solfège syllables directly on the staff. Now that people were expected to read this musical notation, who would teach this skill?

Most of the singing school tradition was found in New England. Singing schools were taught by itinerant teachers (teachers who taught in a town for only a few weeks before moving on to teach in other towns) or by singing masters (the first professional music educators). A typical singing school consisted of fifty students in a class that met in churches, meeting houses, and taverns. Singing masters such as William Billings actually wrote tune books for their singing students. The singing training lasted from one to three months; the end of the instruction was marked by a public demonstration of the students' singing capabilities.

Lowell Mason, musician extraordinaire, composer of sacred music, and president of the Handel and Haydn Society in Boston, headed the "better music movement"—a movement against what he considered the uncultured compositions that most singing masters wrote for inclusion in their tune books for the singing schools' use. (Lowell Mason is also credited with establishing formal music education in the public schools in 1838.)

The purpose of the choral societies (also known as singing societies), such as the Handel and Haydn Society, was to bring master choral works to the public by having them performed by professional and amateur musicians. Also in the mid-1800s, immigrant groups formed their own choral societies (i.e., German-Americans' Deutsche Liederkranz, English glee clubs).

In the twentieth century, a cappella singing became a popular musical trend at prominent colleges and universities, for example, Northwestern University, St. Olaf Lutheran College, Westminster Choir College, and the Harvard Glee Club. Also during the twentieth century, America witnessed the development of many professional and community choral ensembles. Among other developments were high school show choirs and community children's choirs.

Church Choirs

There was little development of the church choir before the 1800s. Typically, people who could read music were seated together during the church service. Eventually, these folks were moved to the front of the church in order to lead others during the church service music. Shakers, the Ephrata Cloister, and the Moravians all contributed to the compositions for and development of choral singing in a church setting.

From camp meetings (Methodist events that occurred on the American frontier lands) evolved American hymns, spirituals, revival songs, Sunday School songs, and contemporary Christian music. This music is of the Protestant hymn and crusade traditions.

The historical context of the North American choral music tradition is that which is predominantly presented in music education history books. The Eurocentric tradition of the East Coast of the North American continent gradually moved westward as new settlements were founded. It is important to recognize that singing was a cultural and religious activity integral to the lives of Native Americans throughout the entire North American continent, prior to the establishment of settlements by Europeans. Early religious leaders from Mexico brought their own unique group singing tradition to Texas, New Mexico, Arizona, and California.

BUILDING A COMPREHENSIVE CHORAL MUSIC EDUCATION CURRICULUM

Michael Mark defines comprehensive musicianship as a "term used to describe the interdisciplinary study of music" (1986, p. 183). Bennett Reimer includes three primary components in his definition of any comprehensive music performance program: (1) "teaching that goes beyond the learning of technical skill"; (2) "refined musical sensitivity and skill so that [teachers'] artistic insight can guide the learnings toward excellent performances"; and (3) "each rehearsal being a music learning experience in and of itself as well as part of a well developed performance curriculum" (1989, p. 199).

The music content standards included in the *National Standards for Arts Education* are guidelines, which, when implemented in a rehearsal setting, can transform a choral music program into a choral music *education* program. The primary focus of a choral program should be the creation and performance of choral music. Should the content of such programs exclude "general music" type activities? Embracing and including the music content standards in a performance program imply that the conductor will expose the performers to a variety of musical behaviors that will enrich the music performance experience. Including activities such as listening, composing, improvising, analyzing, evaluating, and discovering cultural, historical, and related artistic underpinnings provides performers with a deeper and complete relationship to the music they are rehearsing and performing. Imagine how experience in these other musical areas might impact students' interpretation, musical decision making, perception, and affective response to a musical idea as they perform it!

One primary responsibility of choral conductors is to provide their students with opportunities to acquire basic musical knowledge (technique, reading and performing music notation). As music educators, we also have the responsibility to facilitate the development of performers who are independent musical thinkers and players. We are building musicians beyond the preparation for any single concert. Reimer (1989) suggests that music performance is more than a final product, but that we as music educators instill a process, a musical journey, which enhances students' independent abilities to perceive and respond to music they perform or otherwise experience.

You might be asking about the practical logistics of incorporating the music content standards into the choral rehearsal setting, especially when choral directors are faced with rigorous performance schedules set by their school administrations or expected by the community at large. My students have commented, "I support the notion of the national standards in theory, but isn't it easier for a general music specialist to incorporate them into a curriculum than for an instrumental or choral director?" The floodgates for questions open. Other students' concerns include: "How does a choral director include the music content standards when there is so much music and technique to teach and to learn?" "Won't this extra material and activity take up a lot of my rehearsal time?" "How will the student performers react to activities that typically occur in general music class? Won't they just want to play or sing the music?"

It is important to recognize that the music content standards will not all be addressed in every choral rehearsal. Including the music content standards is more than an ensemble director's artificial acquiescence to join the national bandwagon. The music content standards can be incorporated directly during a rehearsal or they can be addressed through the creation of short-term or long-term projects, the bulk of the work that students do outside of the rehearsal setting either as independent or collaborative group work.

It is also worth mentioning that several of the music content standards work well when addressed in tandem. For example, listening to a three-minute musical excerpt during rehearsal time might include listening and analyzing musical elements but also could include a discussion as students critique and evaluate the performance with the addition of historical and cultural context. As one performs a twentieth-century piece of music, the students might listen to and compare recordings of other contemporary pieces while also experiencing nontraditional methods of notating musical sound. The music content standards need not be experienced as single entities.

DEVELOPMENT OF THE SINGING VOICE

Elementary School

Young children in the primary elementary school grades (K–2) begin their vocal training as a part of the general music class experience. Here they explore their vocal capabilities—singing, speaking, whispering, yelling, swooping—and all the expressive qualities that can be produced with each of these individual "voices" (dynamics, tone quality, tempo, articulation, pitch level). The quality of most young singers is very light and somewhat airy, and their singing experiences are best accompanied by visual aides and movement. Typically, children of this age can successfully sing songs having a range of an interval of a perfect fifth (d1–a1).

By the time children are in the upper elementary Grades 3–5, they are ready to explore the difference between singing in their chest and head voices. In Grades 3 and 4, posture and proper breathing are emphasized, the primary vocal instruction still occurring in the general music class. During this time, children's vocal ranges expand beyond an octave. Teachers primarily work on songs that are to be sung in unison, as rounds or canons, partner songs, and echo songs with the addition of ostinati, drones, pedal points, descants. These songs with classroom instrumental accompaniment prepare students to sing harmony in a choral situation.

In many elementary schools, there exists a chorus comprised of students in Grades 4 and/or 5. While vocal instruction continues to be an important facet of general music class instruction, the choral opportunity reinforces technique and provides the opportunity for students to sing as a member of a larger group of performers. Singers at this age possess singing voices that can be clear, pure, and resonant. The development of breath control and the use of head voice remain as important learning and teaching issues. While there might be "uncertain" or "dependent" singers who participate in the elementary school choir, most students progress toward becoming independent singers, capable of singing independent lines of music. Repertoire that is suitable and effective for this age level includes music that involves unison singing, canons and rounds, and two- and three-part songs. Some two- and three-part songs are labeled "SA" (soprano, alto) or "SSA" (soprano 1, soprano 2, alto). A recent trend, however, is for choral composers and publishers to label the various lines as Part I, Part II, and Part III. This change is not insignificant. Instead of labeling students as a soprano or an alto, students are encouraged to interchange parts and to have the opportunity to read lines of music other than their own.

Secondary School

Recently there has been a flurry of interest in the middle school voice, primarily because, for years, choral directors simply did not know how to handle the changing voice, sometimes known as the cambiata voice, within their middle

school choirs. Therefore, many middle school boys discontinued singing in choirs at a time when they needed continued musical development and encouragement.

Males' voices do not magically begin or progress through the physiological change overnight. An observant music teacher can recognize signs of impending change, signs that might become apparent as early as fifth grade. The male voice undergoes the bulk of its radical change between the ages of 12 and 14. It is important for the choral director to group these singers together within the middle school choir and to meet separately with the boys, in order to address issues relevant to their singing voices. Furthermore, it is important that the teacher selects choral literature written especially for the cambiata voice or with a male part having a limited vocal range. Songs labeled SAB (soprano, alto, baritone) might be suitable for older middle school voices, depending in which stages of the vocal change the male students are found. A better choice of music is that labeled SAC (soprano, alto, cambiata), although admittedly this is a more recent and rare categorization.

John Cooksey (1992) defines various stages of development of the male changing voice. The unchanged voice is that of a young elementary school child—pure, clear, resonant soprano head voice. The initial period of voice change (Midvoice I) is signified by the boy's loss of notes in his upper vocal range and by a breathiness that is found in his singing tone quality. The high mutation period (Midvoice II) is the phase in which the boy's voice sounds husky, not resonant, and notes in his upper vocal register are not stable. The climax of mutation and key transition period (Midvoice IIA) is marked by extreme instability in singing high pitches, difficulty in changing registers, difficulty in matching pitches in the middle register, and "pushing" of the voice that often results in a cracking voice. Boys literally need to become acquainted with their new voice. Boys who never had difficulty singing encounter muscle-breath coordination difficulty during the time that their voice is changing. This can cause much frustration, so much encouragement from the choral director is essential! After the climax of the vocal change, the voice begins to settle—although not permanently—into a tenor, baritone, or bass voice. The new baritone phase of vocal change is a stabilizing period, but the young man's voice is not that of an adult baritone. The tone quality is light and relatively thin in most cases, yet more flexible and stable in producing pitches than the cambiata voice. Even during the high school years, a male's voice continues to settle into its true vocal part.

Female voices also change, albeit not as drastically noticeable as in the case of pubescent males. The female singing voice may become breathy and unfocused, even "cracky" in the spoken voice, in eighth and ninth grades. The chest voice can sound very heavy, while the highest tones of the range can be pure and strong. Difficulty might occur in females' manipulation of the voice in order to switch between head, middle, and chest voices. In fact, there might be an increase of vocal "breaks" or transitions between singing registers. Female adolescent singers also experience inconsistent range capabilities (Gackle, 2000).

An interesting assignment that students in a choral methods-type course encounter is vocal interviewing. Their task is to observe choral singers of all ages and note vocal characteristics at each level. Ultimately, the music education majors design vocal interviews and then conduct their interviews with students, ages 14–17. Their task is to describe the interviewee's vocal qualities and characteristics and then to suggest an appropriate placement for the singer within an imaginary choir. Here are some of the descriptions gleaned from their observations and vocal interview descriptions.

Description 1

Donald's voice is rather restricted and slightly nasal when he sings consonants. His sense of pitch is quite accurate—and he is very aware of where notes lie within his own range. This is clearly a student who knows his way around the notes of his voice. Donald was happy to comply with the various vocal tasks I asked of him, though in a typical high school way he never seemed entirely certain of himself. This is reflected in his posture, which I will discuss shortly.

Donald is a bass. In his interview, I took him down to an "e"; this was not difficult for him. His aural memory is decent, though not great. Thus, ideally he would be placed near someone with a slightly better ear, though his is good enough that I imagine it would rarely cause a problem. He is in the postmutational stage of vocal development. As such, it is not surprising to see that while he can comfortably hit all of the notes in his range, he has not yet learned how to produce a pleasing and resonant (but not nasal) sound across his range.

Posture and breath support are lacking in his singing, and I suspect a little bit of work on these would go a long way toward helping him sing properly. When he sings, he sticks his head forward—especially if he is at all unsure of a pitch. It was interesting to note that this pinched quality came not from the upper throat, but from the lower throat—where it was being pushed forward out of alignment. Thus he was able to achieve both a pinched sound and a nasal quality when singing consonants ("Papa picked a pepper Polly put it in her pocket," on DO, DO, MI, MI, SOL, SOL, FA, FA, MI, MI, RE, RE, DO, DO).

There is also a tendency to swallow the "a" vowel of the words "Papa" and "Father." Donald tends to sing it as "aw," but achieves that not by mouth shape, but by swallowing the vowel. Again, posture and breath would probably help get him out of his throat.

Donald has a fairly good sense of pitch, and was able to echo my brief patterns for the most part, until they began to include nondiatonic tritones. This is not surprising (many conservatory students cannot do this), but it would be good to include ear-training of this sort for improved intonation.

Donald's musicality seemed restricted by his technical difficulties. In singing, each note received the same dynamic and timbral shading. Thus, musically before I would deal with anything else, I would practice crescendi and decrescendi, and then be sure to carry that over into rehearsals, discussing how to apply this to phrases, and so on.

Description 2

Dan is a high school sophomore. He dresses neatly and carries himself pretty confidently. After warming up with descending five-note scale pattern (sung on "loo"), he asserts that he is a tenor. His voice appears to have moved beyond the high mutational stage of voice change, and he is gradually gaining a greater grasp of the lower range. He is fairly comfortable singing "g" above middle c, although the timbre changes dramatically. He sings clearly and with good resonance in his lower register. His intonation is excellent, although the pitch becomes a bit sharp (and hoarse) in his upper range.

Description 3

Allison's vocal quality is a bit breathy, darker timbre. She has much more confidence in singing in her middle and lower register. The high part of her range (f—an octave plus above middle c) is very light and breathy, with almost no breath support. She is a senior in high school and has apparently been singing alto throughout her singing experience. I would place her in the middle of the alto section, since she seems to be an enthusiastic leader. She has a confident sound and very good intonation. She definitely needs to work on breath support, posture, and developing fluidity of musical line and focused tone.

By the time students are in high school, they are singing literature that is SATB (soprano, alto, tenor, bass), or SSATB (soprano 1, soprano 2, alto, tenor, bass), or even SACB (soprano, alto, cambiata, baritone/bass). Unison singing is important for singers of all age levels to experience, as it refines listening skills that enable choirs to sound as a vibrant unified voice. Literature selected for choirs should include excellent examples that are representative of traditions from Western and non-Western musics. Each year, the American Choral Directors Association's professional journal, *The Choral Journal*, publishes repertoire lists used in honor choir festivals and solo-ensemble competitions; these lists, along with the journal's monthly review of choral repertoire, are excellent resources for the choral music educators. The configuration of voices of a choral score selected by a conductor is, of course, dependent on the type of choir, the vocal capabilities of individual choir members, and the choral tone procured from the choir as a complete ensemble.

CHOOSING CHORAL LITERATURE

Each year, choral directors audition or "interview" the people and voices that they will potenially work with for a semester or for an entire year. The "interview" provides choral music educators with information that will help them determine the literature that will be rehearsed and performed, the placement of the voices within the choir, the individual and group sound, and the music educational goals and objectives for individuals and the choral ensemble.

A key question for choral music educators to ask themselves as they select choral literature for their ensembles is, "What does this piece teach my students?" The musical concepts that can be taught from the choral pieces that the choir director programs in each concert typically coincide with the choral music curriculum and the teacher's goals and objectives for her/his students. Another point to consider is how the music content standards might be incorported within the variety of musical selections. If the choral ensemble is a venue for developing independent musicianship, then the choral literature that the singers rehearse and perform is the primary tool for learning.

While choral music educators consider the musical worth of each choral piece, they also formulate an overall scheme for an interesting and cohesive choral concert presentation. They try to find a variety of tempi, accompaniments, textures, levels of difficulty, moods, styles, harmonies, tonal centers, languages, keys, texts, and opportunities for student solo performance within a piece of music.

Once the pieces are chosen, there are many methods for arranging the selections so that the program is most effective for singing and most pleasing to the audience's ears. Some choral directors group music according to nearly related tonal centers, related texts, composer, stylistic period, thematic idea (i.e., peace, spring, seasons, patriotism), and chronological order. It is typical to find fun novelty pieces to capture the audience's attention and/or to close a choral segment within a concert.

CHORAL OPPORTUNITIES FOR SINGERS

Depending on the size of the school, the strength of its choral program, and the value placed on the choral program by administration and community, a variety of choral experiences can exist at the secondary school level. Middle school choirs are usually grouped by grade level or by gender (boys choir, girls choir, combined choir, sixth-grade choir). High school choirs, however, are more diverse in the function that the choir plays within the school and community and the type of literature that each choir sings. Here is a list (although not exhaustive) of possible choir opportunities found at the high school level. Perhaps you have experienced other types of choirs that you could add to this list.

Show choir	Vocal jazz ensemble
Madrigal choir	International vocal ensemble
Mixed choir	Women's choir
Concert choir	Men's choir
Touring choir	Freshman choir

Other choral opportunities are provided by local, state, and national choral and music education organizations. Each year, many state chapters of The Music Educators National Conference (MENC) sponsor solo-ensemble competitions. These competitions provide opportunities for vocal soloists and choral ensembles to perform for trained choral adjudicators who provide suggestions for and ratings of the ensembles' performance. There is a solo and choral repertoire list that includes music to be performed at the contest; there is also a sight-singing component in the adjudication process. Other MENC divisions, regions, and state organizations host honor choir festivals. Students from schools within a particular district, region, or state audition in order to participate in the rehearsals/performances. The Organization of American Kodály Educators (OAKE) and the American Choral Directors Association (ACDA) also host honor choral events that typically occur during the organizations' regional and national meetings.

AUTHENTIC ASSESSMENT OF A CHORAL SINGER

Portfolios serve as an opportunity for the assessment of individual student efforts, for student and teacher reflection, for program assessment, and for an exhibition of final products and works in progress. Portfolio assessment is a type of assessment that encourages students to become reflective about their own work. Portfolios enable the viewing and reviewing of students' progress throughout the class.

Throughout a grading period—trimester, semester, quarter—students have the opportunity to track their progress. In the process, they refine their ability to recognize their strengths and those areas in which improvement was necessary. Although the students are given the opportunity to assess their own progress, teachers do not relinquish their responsibility for learning. Instead, both student and teacher roles are aligned so that they *share* responsibility for learning (Kerchner, 1996). Teachers, students, and parents meet to discuss musical progress throughout a grading period. Portfolios provide a fairly complete picture of students' progress in vocal and musical skill development, critical thinking skill development, musical preference, and special musical interests. A letter grade on a report card tends not to reflect the complexity of musical and thinking skill development.

Technology can be used to assist singers as they accumulate, organize, and maintain items including videotapes, journals, reflections, audiotapes, concert programs, and rehearsal reviews, concert reviews, compositions, written warmups, and written tests for their portfolio collection. Software programs such as HyperStudio and HyperCard support a variety of data forms, including videotape and audiotape input. Students can enter written information directly into the program. Since portfolios can be cumbersome for teachers to store in a music classroom, a CD-ROM version of the portfolio is a practical solution for maintaining student assessment data.

CHORAL LESSON PLAN

I. **Grade Level/Class:** Middle school SAB choir (Grade 8)

II. **Musical Concept:** Melodic theme recognition

(Prior knowledge: read-through of "Hosanna in Excelsis" by Orlando di Lasso)

III. **National Standard(s) Addressed:**

Singing (1), reading/notating music (5), listening to/analyzing/describing (6)

continued

IV. Learning Outcome/Objective

Students will be able to . . .

- sing primary motivic material of "Hosanna" on "doo"
- stand each time they sing the primary motivic idea
- circle the primary motivic material in "Hosanna" score
- identify the order of voices in which motivic material is presented while listening to a recording

V. Materials needed for lesson (for student and teacher):

Piano, "Hosanna in Excelsis" by Orlando di Lasso, stereo system, CD of Mozart: "Kyrie" (*Requiem*), pencils

VI. Teaching Procedures (activities AND questions) (Time: twelve minutes)

1. Teacher will sing alto line (primary motivic material) on "doo"; students will echo teacher.

   Q: Where is this musical idea first found in "Hosanna"?

   Q: Who can describe the movement of this melodic idea, its contour? (Teacher introduces the term "motivic idea.")

2. Students sing "Hosanna" (on "doo") and stand each time they sing the primary motivic material.

3. Students circle in their score each time they note a voice part that sings the primary motivic material.

   Q: What is the order in which the motivic material is presented?

4. Teacher sings "Kyrie" theme from Mozart "Kyrie" (*Requiem*); students echo teacher.

5. Teacher plays CD recording of Mozart "Kyrie" (*Requiem*). Students raise hand each time they hear "Kyrie" and mark on a piece of paper which voice sings the "Kyrie" theme.

6. Discuss student responses (order of vocal "Kyrie" entrances).

   Q: Why do you think a composer might use this imitation of melodic motive and use it repeatedly? What effect does it create?

   Q: Is that the only material that occurs? Describe what else goes on. (Go back to "Hosanna" score.)

   Q: Why wouldn't a composer use only the melodic motivic material?

VII. Lesson Evaluation

DISCUSSION OF LESSON PLAN

1. Which music content standards in the National Standards for Music are addressed in this lesson plan (see Introduction for Music Content Standards listing)?
2. With regard to the sequence of the lesson, why did the teacher consider it an effective sequence to have the students sing and physically move as they sang the motivic material?
3. Is this lesson teacher-directed, student-directed, or a shared learning partnership? Explain your response.
4. Consider the other music content standards. In future rehearsals of this choral piece, how would you incorporate the other music content standards that are not already evident in the lesson?
5. What is the significance of the teacher asking "open-ended" questions? How might these questions lead to musical discovery and conceptual learning?
6. Why did the conductor decide to include the Mozart listening example—a piece of music that was not being rehearsed by the choir? How did it fit into the lesson? How might student responses to this activity lead to the teacher's informal assessment of the singers' music learning during this particular rehearsal?

QUESTIONS FOR DISCUSSION

1. How might a choral director retain male participation in a secondary school's choral program during their cambiata years?
2. You are meeting with a school administrator. You are asked to justify your reasons for wanting your choirs to meet during the school day. Why should your choirs meet during the school day? What is your rationale?
3. How does a choral program gain school, student, parent, and community support?
4. Should singers in your choir experience both sacred and secular music? Why or why not?

FOLLOWUP ASSIGNMENTS

1. Observe a choral rehearsal at the elementary, middle school, and/or high school level. Use verbal descriptors (metaphors) to describe the vocal quality of the choral sound at each level.

2. Observe a choral rehearsal. Using the adapted "Flander's Interaction Analysis Matrix" (p. 26), mark on the grid the type of verbal and nonverbal interaction that transpires between the choral director and her/his singers.

3. Choose a piece of choral music. Create warmups that would fit challenging areas of the piece you have chosen. Sketch the means that you would use in order to incorporate each of the National Standards for Music.

REFERENCES

Books and Articles

COOKSEY, J. (1992). *Working with the Adolescent Voice*. St. Louis, MO: Concordia.

FLANDERS, N. (1970). *Analyzing Teacher Behavior*. Reading, MA: Addison-Wesley.

GACKLE, L. (2000). "Female Adolescent Voice Transformations, Book 5, Chapter 5." In Thurman, L. and Welch, G. (eds.), *Body, Mind and Voice: Foundations of Voice Education*. Iowa City, IA: National Center for Voice and Speech.

KERCHNER, J. (1996). "Portfolio Assessment: Tracking Development." *Journal of Music Teacher Education*, 6(2), pp. 19–22.

MARK, M. (1986). *Contemporary Music Education* (second ed.). New York: Schirmer.

REIMER, B. (1989). *A Philosophy of Music Education*. Englewood Cliffs, NJ: Prentice Hall.

Valuable Resources

COLLINS, D. (1993). *Teaching Choral Music*. Englewood Cliffs, NJ: Prentice Hall.

HYLTON, J. (1995). *Comprehensive Choral Music Education*. Englewood Cliffs, NJ: Prentice Hall.

JORDAN, J. (1996). *Evoking Sound*. Chicago, IL: GIA Publications.

PHILLIPS, K. (1992). *Teaching Kids to Sing*. New York: Schirmer.

RAO, D. (1993). *We will Sing!* New York: Boosey and Hawkes.

Valuable Internet Resources

ChoralNet
<http://www.choralnet.org>

International Federation for Choral Music
<http://www.sdsmt.edu/choralnet>

Pepper National Music Network (PNMN)
<http://www.jwpepper.com>

Professional Associations

American Choral Directors Association (ACDA)
502 SW 38th Street
Lawton, OK 73505
508-355-8161
<http://acdaonline.org>

International Society for Music Education (ISME)
International Office
P.O. Box 909
Medlands 6909, WA
Australia
++61-(0)8-9386-2654
<http://www.isme.org>

Music Educators National Conference (MENC)
The National Association for Music Education
1806 Robert Fulton Drive
Reston, VA 20191
800-336-3768
<http://www.menc.org

Adapted from "Flanders Interaction Analysis Matrix"
(Check the frequency of each behavior within a 10–15 minute period of observation)

Exhibited Choral Director's Behaviors While Rehearsing:

Feelings/Emotions																							
Affirmation of students																							
Probing student responses (asking for additional explanation)																							
Using student ideas																							
Music performance/ demonstration																							
Wait time for student response																							
Asking divergent questions (higher-order thinking)																							
Asking convergent questions (yes/no; recall; lower-level thinking)																							
Lecture																							
Directions																							
Criticism																							
Silence (other than wait time for student response)																							
Nonverbal response to students																							

(Flanders, 1970, p. 88)

9

Multicultural Music Education

Mrs. Umber began the fourth grade music class by asking, "What is a powwow?" In the previous lesson, the class had performed a Kiowa round dance/song from the Southern Plains powwow tradition, discussed the meaning and usage of the round dance, found the Kiowa Indians on a map of Indian nations, watched video clips, and read books about powwows. Student responses to Mrs. Umber's question included these: "When a group of people get together to do dances and contests, drumming, and wear the costumes they make," "showing appreciation of their culture," "when they get to see people they haven't seen in a long time, to visit with each other and to find out who got married," "food, stories, arts and crafts," "it's basically a party, to celebrate," "they have a tournament of dances," "they play instruments and sing," "when a bunch of Indians from different tribes get together—for social reasons, to show they're real proud of their tribe." One student added, "They become the 'drum.'" The teacher added that a powwow provides tradition and a sense of community, remembering who you are. The teacher talked about the use of the word "costume" and the fact that an Indian she knew, Tree Cody, said, "On Halloween you wear a costume to be something you're not. We're Indian. We don't wear a 'costume.'" The teacher said to use the word "regalia" instead and wrote this word on the board. The students listened attentively. When the teacher also announced that there was a local powwow that weekend at the university's marching band field, one student said, "I'm going!" and another said, "Me, too!" Several students wanted directions to the powwow.

The teacher explained that in today's lesson students would learn some powwow drumming, various patterns containing "hard beats" or accents, and the custom that good dancers at a powwow must stop on the very last beat of the drum. Mrs. Umber divided the class into small groups to take turns playing the powwow drumming patterns. The first group had trouble with the pattern 1 2 3 4 5 and 1 2 3 4 5, having a tendency to fall into the stereotypical pattern of 1 2 3 4 1 2 3 4. Another small group had trouble with the pattern 1 2 3 4 5 6 7, after which the teacher said, "Yes, it's not so easy. You thought Native American drumming was easy, but this is hard for you." All groups had difficulty with the pattern 1 2 3 4 5 6 7 8 9 and the teacher said, "This one was the hardest one for every class." When the students lapsed into the 1 2 3 4 1 2 3 4 pattern Mrs. Umber said, "That's what they [Indians] *don't* do—have you figured that out? Do you see that pattern up there anywhere? No." The teacher showed the class a picture of Indian powwow drummers. One student commented that the drummers were wearing cowboy hats, to which the teacher replied, "Yes. This shows both traditional and modern that way, doesn't it?" The teacher then said, "There's a game that goes with this [drumming]. Can you handle it? You [the dancers] have to stop on the last beat of the drum." Students expressed excitement and anticipation, eagerly playing the "game."

The class got somewhat noisy using the drum and had some difficulty performing the accented beats correctly but appeared to enjoy themselves. Several students made comments such as, "Do we get another chance to play?" Will we get to play it again?" The class applauded when one small group played their pattern correctly. When another group played correctly, both teacher and students said a resounding "Yes!" in approval. When the children had difficulty, the teacher said, "Yes—it's not easy." Several groups problem-solved in order to start together, using phrases such as, "Ready, go," or "Follow me." Mrs. Umber had the class play the same "game" of moving/dancing but stopping on the last drumbeat. She played a recording of powwow drumming and singing for the class. Afterward the teacher said, "Now you know Indian music doesn't go 1234 1234. Now you know."

As the fourth grade class left the music room, Mrs. Umber felt a sense of satisfaction. Reflecting on her own elementary school experiences with American Indian[1] cultures, she remembered singing "Ten Little Indians" and participating in a Thanksgiving play in which she sat "Indian style." She was glad some things had improved!

WHAT IS MULTICULTURAL EDUCATION? HOW DOES IT APPLY TO MUSIC EDUCATION?

The preceding scenario depicts a multicultural music lesson. The term "multicultural"[2] can be problematic, for it means many things to many people. Many educators see multiculturalism as a broad spectrum with assimilation (relinquishing one's own culture or merging it with a "dominant" culture) at one end of the spectrum and cultural pluralism or cultural diversity (in which each person's culture is honored, valued, and respected) at the other end. There are undoubtedly as many points along the spectrum as there are approaches to multiculturalism.

> Multicultural education is by definition expansive. Because it is *about* all people, it is also *for* all people, regardless of their ethnicity, language, religion, gender, race, or class. It can even be convincingly argued that students from the dominant culture

[1]For purposes of this chapter, the terms "American Indian," "Native American," and "Indian" will be used interchangeably to mean North American Indian.

[2]For purposes of this chapter, the terms "multicultural" and "multiethnic" will be used interchangeably to mean diverse global/world cultures.

need multicultural education more than others, for they are often the most miseducated about diversity in our society. In fact, European American youths often feel that they do not even *have* a culture, at least not in the same sense that clearly culturally identifiable youths do. At the same time, they feel that their way of living, of doing things, of believing, and of acting are simply the only possibilities. Anything else is ethnic and exotic. (Nieto, 1996, p. 313)

The internationally known expert Geneva Gay (1994) defines multicultural education as "the policies, programs, and practices employed in schools to celebrate cultural diversity" (p. 3). Patricia Shehan Campbell (1992), an expert on multiculturalism applied to music education, labels "multicultural" as the common term used to describe a music program that emphasizes a world view.

A Brief History of Multicultural Music Education

Multiculturalism is currently a major topic in the music education (and general education) profession, but the idea is not new. National symposia at Yale University in 1963, Tanglewood in 1967, and Wesleyan in 1984 launched the topic of multicultural music to prominence in the profession. Multicultural music education has been the central theme of many international and national conferences of prominent professional organizations such as the Music Educators National Conference (MENC), International Society for Music Education (ISME), The College Music Society (CMS), and the American Orff-*Schulwerk* Association (AOSA), as well as regional and state in-service events. Multicultural music education, perhaps due to its very nature, is an area of collaboration among music educators, classroom teachers, ethnomusicologists, anthropologists, and sociologists. Such landmark collaborative efforts as the 1990 Symposium on Multicultural Approaches to Music Education are testimony to the renewed interest in this topic, as are the formation of the Society for Ethnomusicology (SEM)'s Education Committee and the AOSA's Multicultural Music Education Committee, among others.

Educational Philosophy and Rationale: Why Include World Musics in the Classroom?

The MENC adopted a resolution on future directions and actions at the 1990 Symposium on Multicultural Approaches to Music Education, documented in *Teaching Music with a Multicultural Approach* (Anderson, 1991). One of the document's eleven resolutions is that "music teachers will seek to assist students in understanding that there are many different but equally valid forms

of musical expression" (p. 90). This can prevent closed views toward other ways of making music. An educational philosophy and rationale for including world musics in curriculum does not rely on promoting world peace for its purpose but, rather, "because these musics are there, and studying them will immeasurably broaden both our musical and our cultural understanding" (Nettl, 1992, p. 6). Indeed, might it be each child's *right* to learn and experience many forms of musical expression?

Think about your reactions to the following two statements: (1) Music is a universal language; (2) America is a cultural melting pot. In her chapter of the *Handbook of Research on Music Teaching and Learning,* "Multicultural Music Education in a Pluralistic Society," Joyce Jordan (1992) illuminated the search for a philosophic base for multicultural music education. She considered these two statements to be common misconceptions about ethnic diversity and musical expression.

Perhaps you have thought of other metaphors you prefer to "melting pot," such as a "tossed salad," "stew," "quilt," or "mosaic." You also might have thought of terms you prefer to "universal language," such as universal "phenomenon," "response," "expression," or simply "a universal."

Our classroom populations are more diverse than ever. Part of being prepared to be a music teacher today is to have experience teaching with a multicultural perspective.

The predictions for multiethnic and multiracial population increases in the United States in the next century are staggering, and our country will become even more of a microcosm of the world than it is today. We must be ready for the fact, and music teachers and music programs must be even more prepared to teach about the strengths of multicultural diversity through music than ever before. (Olsen, 2000, p. 16)

Classroom Teaching and Curricular Approaches

What are some effective ways to incorporate world musics in our music classroom curriculum? How can we take our students from the "known" to the "unknown"? One way is to link the music to our curriculum through the musical elements themselves—for example, pitch, rhythm, form, tone color. The "common elements" approach appears to be the mainstay of teaching world musics to children and is prevalent in the literature. In this approach, the common musical elements such as rhythm, melody, or form are identified in each type of music studied; however, this approach can be overused and may not apply to all musics.

Multicultural music can be readily utilized in the general music classroom. As music study for all students in a school, general music curricula can appropriately incorporate diverse music in instruction. But expansion to other areas of music education not previously considered as viable "vehicles" for multicultural education has occurred as well. Ways to incorporate multicultural music in band[3] or orchestra concerts, and suggested multicultural resources for a choral program are found in the May 1992 issue of *Music Educators Journal*, among other sources. If a band is learning the piece "Variations on a Korean Folk Song," for instance, the band director might have the students learn to sing the original folk song on which the work is based, and have students look on the World Wide Web for information on Korea to provide some cultural context. The band might learn about Korean folk instruments or Korean ensembles. A high school orchestra might learn about string instruments in Mexican mariachi ensembles and perform a piece in one of those styles. Not only can choirs learn pieces from diverse cultures, they also can hear authentic examples, learn the circumstances under which the pieces are sung, and then perform them in styles that fit the specific cultures. High quality multicultural teaching materials for all areas of multicultural teaching have proliferated in recent years.

MENC (1994) addressed multicultural music in the National Standards. Three of the nine national voluntary content standards in music directly or indirectly include learning music of diverse cultures, particularly standard number 9, "Understanding music in relation to history and culture." The document calls for a new music curriculum that uses a variety of music within each genre or culture in order to avoid musical stereotyping.

---

[3]For further information the reader is referred to the article by Volk, T. (2002). "An Annotated List of Multicultural Music for Band." *TRIAD* (May/June), 69(6), pp. 24–26.

A list of achievement standards is presented for each of the nine content standards. "Genres and styles of diverse cultures" is included within the achievement standards four times in addition to the following: (1) identifying the sounds of instruments from various cultures, (2) describing how elements of music are used in music from various cultures of the world, and (3) identifying and describing roles of musicians in various cultures.

In addition to instruction for purely artistic or musical goals, multicultural music has been integrated with other subject areas through the use of small-group work and active, "hands-on" learning. The scenario at the beginning of this chapter is an example of an active learning approach. The lesson plan and its adaptation for a student-directed small-group strategy are found at the end of this chapter.

Multicultural Music in the Classroom: Challenges and Benefits

What are some of the problems, obstacles, or challenges with regard to the inclusion of multicultural music in our teaching? You can probably think of several. One challenge involves authenticity and presentation. How can you evaluate whether a resource is authentic?

A checklist for evaluating multicultural music teaching materials was devised by Judith C. Tucker (1992) in conjunction with the Society for Ethnomusicology (SEM) Education Committee. Some important considerations indicative of authenticity are that the materials were prepared with the involvement of someone within the culture, arrangements or accompaniments have minimal or no adaptation, lyrics are presented in the original language, and a cultural context for each piece is included.

We hear the term "cultural context" often with regard to presenting world musics; educators must be conscious of the importance of *cultural context* in learning about or teaching multicultural music. Consider cultural context as knowing "who, where, why, how, and when" regarding the music, preserving its integrity and authenticity. With regard to cultural context for a selected song, multicultural music specialist Ellen McCullough-Brabson (1995) suggested that teachers find out who traditionally performs the song, if it is gender-specific, associated with certain times of the year or day, what the meaning is of the song, whether social values or norms are connected with the song, and what style of singing is used for performing the song.

Another challenge that can pose a dilemma is finding time within our curriculum. Should we include many world musics as a "smorgasboard" approach or fewer musics in a more in-depth way that crosses many areas of the general curriculum? Perhaps some of you learned world music as part of an "Around the World" music unit in the spring to correlate with your school's

cultural fair or other event. Generally it is more meaningful for students to do less breadth and more depth. You can weave multicultural music into your curriculum throughout the year rather than only during one unit or for one concert. Instead of choosing music for an "extrinsic" justification (for example, Native American music for Thanksgiving or African-American music for Black History Month), it is helpful and less of a "token" experience to include multicultural music throughout the year for musical reasons.

What are some of the benefits of teaching multicultural music? Many are probably obvious to you already. Perhaps many of you reading this chapter have benefited personally from world music study and performance. Children enjoy learning many musical styles and becoming "musically flexible" or "polymusical."

Implications for Instruction: An Example from Research

Results of research by Kay Edwards (1998) provided new information regarding both process and product for multicultural music instruction. As a direct result of a two-year project, critical pedagogical points were articulated that can apply to the teaching of other world musics:

1. Music educators can *start large, then work small.* Begin with "the big picture" by teaching the variety of a country or culture's music with an overview of many musical styles (traditional and contemporary); then, utilize a culture-specific approach.

2. Many sound pedagogical approaches currently being used to teach elementary general music work well with teaching world musics; perhaps the most critical of these is *active learning through a variety of learning experiences.* "Hands-on" opportunities to sing, play instruments, dance, move, read, listen, and watch all comprise successful instruction with world music and serve to facilitate an understanding of *cultural context.* High quality, successful experiences may require considerable *instructional time* to avoid "token" curricular inclusion.

3. Pedagogical approaches currently being used in the regular classroom (perhaps more often than in the music classroom) also lend themselves well to instruction in world music. For instance, *learning centers* (individual "stations" set up in scattered places around the room) and *cooperative learning strategies* (group work where each person has a job and all are accountable) provide students a sense of ownership within a more student-directed "discovery" approach as compared to only using a large-group "traditional" approach; use a variety of teaching techniques.

4. Quality instructional materials are of the utmost importance. Whenever possible, authentic (native) instruments should be utilized. *Authenticity* of all instructional materials should be a paramount consideration—including recordings, songs, photographs, and books. When imitations must be used, let the children know that the item is only "similar" to the real thing. Seek advice from "cultural insiders" or other experts regarding authenticity and appropriateness of instructional materials.

5. Correlate with existing curriculum to provide children with an even greater perceived purpose for learning. Work with the classroom teacher and others to correlate multicultural music with social studies, literature, art, or physical education (e.g., dance), thus highlighting the interconnectedness/integration of music, dance, and culture.

6. Relevance to the child's world is critical for a depth of learning to take place beyond superficial experiences with any culture. One successful approach is to provide a bridge for student learning from the "known" to the "unknown" through the use of contemporary music in addition to traditional music. You may wish to select materials that are based on native peoples who live or once lived in the school's geographic area. If possible, arrange for guest artists who represent local cultural groups to visit the classroom. Tell students about local public events.

7. Utilize both *traditional and contemporary music* in instruction to show students that a culture's music is not static, but constantly evolving—and to provide

further relevance to the child's world. Bulletin board items and other instructional media (such as videos) can also highlight both traditional and contemporary lifeways.

8. A *guest artist* provides an "insider's view" of a culture that no other form of world music instruction can. It is important for children to know a culture's people and to know about their music firsthand. Having the chance to meet with and talk to a guest artist (at least from a video if not in person) can help dispel stereotypes and provide correct information quickly. Have specific instructional goals and criteria for selecting the guest artist; consider organizing a panel to make the selection based on the goals and criteria. Consult the selected guest artist or other special guests in your school or community regarding the selection and authenticity of instructional materials. Music teachers should not expect a guest artist to be a trained music teacher, but step back and allow the culture bearer to instruct children in his/her own manner; it may be that the culture bearer's presence and message will compensate for any perceived instructional flaws.

9. *Music teacher preparation* in multicultural music must include adequate time for preparation and assimilation of new musical styles. If possible, take a course on world music. One-on-one multicultural music education "mentoring" in the study of another culture's music (by a colleague experienced in a particular culture's music/dance) is one effective approach.

10. As a teacher, work to *dispel cultural and musical stereotypes* at every opportunity (for example, pay careful attention to phrases used in everyday teaching such as "sitting pretzel-style" or "criss-cross" instead of "Indian-style"). The words we choose and the expectations we have as educators greatly influence the attitudes of our students. Guide students to think of world musics as "interesting," "unusual," "exciting," or "different," rather than "strange" or "weird."

Some of these same tips for successful teaching are noted by McCullough-Brabson (1995): (1) use the language of the culture; (2) provide translations; (3) use authentic materials; (4) know the cultural context; (5) develop respect for other cultures; (6) avoid words with negative stereotyping; (7) know the meaning of songs; and (8) sing in the vocal style of the culture. The research and work of many in the field of multicultural music education[4] indicate that students of all ages can develop cultural sensitivities that extend beyond mere knowledge and perhaps reach the heart.

---

[4]For further information and resources, the reader is referred to MENC's sourcebook, *Multicultural Perspectives in Music Education,* by Anderson and Campbell (1989 and 1996).

WHAT DOES ALL THIS MEAN FOR YOU AS A FUTURE MUSIC TEACHER?

It is likely that the students in your future classroom will have diverse musical backgrounds, interests, and needs. Your preparation for this is paramount. It is validating to know that by including world musics in your teaching, you will be fulfilling the MENC National Standards for Music. MENC's resolutions for future directions in teaching multicultural music include that such teaching will: (1) be incorporated into every elementary and secondary music curriculum and will include experiences in singing, playing instruments, listening, creative activity, and movement/dance; (2) be incorporated in all educational settings including general, instrumental, and choral music education; (3) include both intensive and comparative experiences in world musics; (4) include the cultural context of the music studied; and (5) support the "broadest manifestations of musical expression" through the development of appropriate concepts and terminology (Anderson, 1991, p. 90).

This can all seem overwhelming to beginning teachers. But for any of you interested in being a musically inclusive teacher, there are several simple ways to begin your journey.

Ways to Get Started

Each of you reading this has a cultural background and experience to share. Each of your students will have one (or more) as well. Culture is *learned* and may be different from a person's ethnicity or race. As you develop rapport with your students you will find appropriate and respectful ways to allow them to share their musical or cultural experiences if they desire.

One of the best ways to begin incorporating multicultural music into your teaching is to draw upon local resources in your school and your community. Attend cultural events, go to museums, listen and learn from what is right there in your environment. Invite guest artists to your school. Various artist-in-residence programs are available through grants from state and local arts agencies; these can provide more in-depth learning about a culture and its music. Attend workshops, conferences, and other events sponsored by MENC and other professional music organizations. Take a course in world music or participate in an ethnic music ensemble. Seek out quality resources from catalogs such as World Music Press[5]; look especially for resources produced by "cultural insiders" or in conjunction with culture bearers. In your own travels, take time to experience local music traditions and to meet musicians. Read books, watch videos, and listen to authentic recordings of specific cultures' music. Acquire authentic instruments for use in your classroom or approxi-

---

[5] World Music Press <http://www.worldmusicpress.com>

mate an instrumental sound the best you can; when you do so, explain to students the difference between the authentic version and the adapted version, whether it be the sound of an instrument or of an entire ensemble.

Incorporating the music of the whole world is quite a formidable task (!), and actually may not be as valuable to our students as more in-depth experiences. As Patricia Shehan Campbell (1992) has suggested, we can begin by becoming "bimusical." We likely find that within any one culture's music there are many styles, both traditional and contemporary. There are many contemporary fusions of native styles such as classical, country, rap, and others.

Many schools sponsor multicultural festivals for the community that may feature a formal music/dance concert as its centerpiece but may also include foods, visual arts, and stories. Local ethnic groups from the community can be showcased as well as student performances. In choosing a format for such a festival, the simplest approach may be to plan a series of visits to the classroom by performers from the community; presentations for the entire school could be part of a schoolwide integrated curriculum. Bryan Burton (1992) stressed that the purpose of multicultural presentations is a sharing of culture rather than a polished, professional performance.

Technology constantly provides us with world resources. For example, choral music educator Mary Goetze and Jay Fern have produced a set of CD-ROMs set on choral music from diverse cultures. There also are CD-ROMs on musical instruments of the world and other related topics in ethnomusicology. Use technology to provide you with additional information regarding the countries/cultures of the music you teach.

CLOSING THOUGHTS

In her book *Affirming Diversity*, Sonia Nieto (1996) states, "Curriculum and materials represent the *content* of multicultural education, but multicultural education is above all a *process*" (p. 317). Although the inclusion of multicultural music in curriculum presents challenges to today's educators, the benefits are many. As global music becomes more pervasive on a daily basis, our repertoire of "classroom music" reflects more of "real world" music and thereby can provide important connections for all of our students.

As new music educators of the twenty-first century, you have the opportunity to be better prepared than previous generations to teach diverse populations utilizing diverse musics.

> Cultural diversity is a fact of human existence; we must recognize that fact and we must teach music in a way that reflects the virtues and values of all cultures in our global village (earth) and our continental village (USA). The variety of humanity's creations and expressions is one of humanity's greatest strengths, and not to teach about multicultural diversity through music would be to backslide—a very dangerous prospect. (Olsen, 2000, p. 16)

SAMPLE LESSON AND SMALL-GROUP TEACHING STRATEGIES

BEAT/ACCENT
LISTENING/PLAYING
Grades 4–8

Lesson: POWWOW DRUMMING

Recording: "Medium Fast War Dance heading into Fast Contest Dance" from *Powwow: Central Plains Club of Phoenix, AZ* (Canyon Records, 1972) or "Chief Mountain" from *Powwow Highway Songs* (Black Lodge Singers)

National Standard: 9

(APPLICABLE STATE STANDARDS)

Concept: An accent is "something different" in the music's basic beat, allowing certain beats to "stick out." Patterns of accents are used in Plains Powwow music.

Objective: Students will listen to recordings of Plains powwow music. Students will play various accent patterns and show the accents with movement, stopping on the last drumbeat.

Materials: (1) recording; (2) large powwow drums (bass drums okay); (3) mallets/beaters; (4) chalkboard

Sequence: Open the session by writing "con-DUCT" and "CON-duct" on the board and discussing different ways of saying the same word. Invite students to give examples of various accents in speaking. Correlate to music by saying that just as an accent in speaking is "something different," likewise in music an accent is something different, making beats "stick out."

1. (optional) Practice with sets of numbers 1–8, having students select numbers for beat to be accented, circling the different combinations. Clap the accented patterns; play them on instruments; move by stepping all eight counts and clapping on the accented ones; switch.

2. Divide the students into groups of five to eight, having them sit around a large drum, powwow style. Show them a picture of Native American drummers/singers sitting this way. Tell them that a "drum" refers to the entire group around each drum. Explain that a powwow is an Indian festival with dance contests, food, and crafts. Attend one as a field trip if possible. (If you do not have enough drums, other students can be movers/dancers; switch off.)

continued

3. Play the pattern <u>1</u> 2 <u>3</u> 4 <u>5</u> . Have students guess which beats were accented. Invite them to play the pattern. Move by stepping on all counts and clapping on accents; switch.

4. Have each group (or one person from each group) choose accented beats using 1 2 3 4 5 to play for the class; other groups guess.

5. Explain that <u>1</u> 2 <u>3</u> 4 <u>5</u> is a traditional powwow drumming pattern. If the last accent is very strong, it signals the end of the song. Try it. Play steady beats with no accents, then use the five-beat pattern while someone else dances or improvises on a gourd rattle. To signal the end of the piece, make the last beat very loud.

6. Play the other five-beat ending patterns: <u>1</u> 2 <u>3</u> <u>4</u> <u>5</u> and <u>1</u> <u>2</u> <u>3</u> 4 <u>5</u>. Have students identify the accented beats; have others move.

7. Listen to examples of these patterns using the recordings of powwow drumming. (The music often continues after these patterns; they are not ostinati or a meter of five.)

8. Try the seven-beat ending pattern: <u>1</u> 2 <u>3</u> <u>4</u> <u>5</u> <u>6</u> <u>7</u>. Listen to examples.

9. Try the nine-beat ending pattern: <u>1</u> 2 <u>3</u> <u>4</u> <u>5</u> <u>6</u> <u>7</u> 8 <u>9</u>. Listen/move.

10. Challenge: Have students identify the accented beats in the "hot five" eleven-beat drumming style: <u>1</u> 2 3 4 <u>5</u> 6 <u>7</u> 8 <u>9</u> 10 <u>11</u>. Play the pattern.

11. Show the musical symbol for an accent (if you haven't already). Explain that these accented beats are also called "honor beats" by Native Americans.

Questions/Closure:	Tell your neighbor what a powwow is. Have them tell you one of the accented patterns we played today.
Evaluation:	Check for beat competency and accuracy of accented beat patterns.
Extension:	Organize an all-school or grade-level powwow! Attend a powwow.

* * * * * * * * * *

General Information: Southern Plains-style powwow drumming is usually set up with one main "drum" in the center of the dance arena. Northern Plains-style is usually set up with several "drums" around the outside of the arena. Both styles have been adapted by local powwows.

> Each dancer's individuality is expressed by his or her regalia (special outfit), and each part of the regalia is special. Regalia are often passed down through family generations. There are contests for all age groups, male and female, at powwows.

LEARNING CENTER: POWWOW DRUMMING (SMALL GROUP STRATEGY)

Materials: Drum, mallets, headphones, books, recordings

1. Listen to the powwow drumming tapes using your headphones. Play along, matching the accented "honor" beats. Use other tapes that are at the center, doing the same thing.
2. Read about powwows in the books at this learning center such as *A Trip to a Pow Wow* by Richard Red Hawk (Sacramento, CA: Sierra Oaks Publishing Co., 1988).
3. Look at the powwow photographs at the center.
4. Rewind the tapes when you are finished.

QUESTIONS FOR DISCUSSION

1. What are some of the benefits of teaching world musics?
2. What experiences have you had with other cultures and their music?
3. What types of multicultural projects were you involved in during your school years? Which were most meaningful to you and why?

FOLLOWUP ACTIVITIES/ASSIGNMENTS

1. Share your "cultural roots" with a class member and share music examples.
2. Interview someone from a cultural background different than your own. Write your findings.

REFERENCES

ANDERSON, W. and CAMPBELL, P. (eds.) (1989, 1996). *Multicultural Perspectives in Music Education* (first and second eds.). Reston, VA: MENC.

ANDERSON, W. M., Jr. (1991). *Teaching Music with a Multicultural Approach*. Reston, VA: MENC.

BURTON, B. (1992). "Multicultural Festivals: Extensions of General Music." *General Music Today*, 5(3), pp. 17–18.

CAMPBELL, P. S. (1992). "Cultural Consciousness in Teaching General Music." *Music Educators Journal*, 78(9), pp. 30–3.

EDWARDS, K. L. (1998). "Multicultural Music in the Elementary School: What Can be Achieved?" *Bulletin of the Council for Research in Music Education*, Fall (138), pp. 62–82.

GAY, G. (1994). *At the Essence of Learning: Multicultural Education*. West Lafayette, IN: Kappa Delta Pi.

JORDAN, J. (1992). "Multicultural Music Education in a Pluralistic Society." In R. Colwell (ed.), *Handbook of Research on Music Teaching and Learning* (pp. 735–45). New York: Macmillan, Inc./MENC.[6]

McCULLOUGH-BRABSON, E. (1995). "Music and Cultural Diversity: Thoughts from a World Music Cheerleader." In S. Stauffer (ed.), *Toward Tomorrow: New Visions for General Music* (pp. 75–80). Reston, VA: MENC.

MENC. (1994). *The School Music Program, A New Vision: The K–12 National Standards, PreK Standards, and What They Mean to Music Educators.* Reston, VA: Author.

NETTL, B. (1992). "Ethnomusicology and the Teaching of World Music." *International Journal of Music Education*, 22, pp. 3–7.

NIETO, S. (1996). *Affirmity Diversity: The Sociopolitical Context of Multicultural Education* (second ed.). White Plains, NY: Longman.

OLSEN, D. (2000). "The President's Comments." In *Newsletter of The College Music Society*, January, p. 16.

RED HAWK, R. (1988). *A Trip to a Pow Wow.* Sacramento, CA: Sierra Oaks Publishing Co.

TUCKER, J. C. (1992). "Circling the Globe: Multicultural Resources." *Music Educators Journal*, 78(9), pp. 37–40.

---

[6]For further information, the reader is referred to Barbara Reeder Lundquist's chapter, "Music, Culture, Curriculum, and Instruction," in Colwell, R. and Richardson, C. (eds.). (2002). *The New Handbook of Research on Music Teaching and Learning.* New York: Oxford University Press/MENC, pp. 626–647.

10

Including Diverse Learners

EXCEPTIONAL LEARNERS

As the second graders entered the music room, they showed much energy and excitement in their body movement, facial gestures, and vocal sounds. Some children walked, some hopped, some skipped, some held hands of other children as they arrived through the doorway. They knew that on entering Mr. Nevan's classroom that they were to sit in a circle on the carpeted floor. The last student to enter the classroom came on a wheelchair that was pushed by a teacher's assistant. The little girl in the wheelchair turned her head from side to side, thrashing her long blonde hair in front of her face. Her vocal sounds did not formulate words or sentences, but rather seemingly involuntary swoops and abrupt "uh" interjections. Braces contained her legs to a single position, while her one arm was raised to a position just below her chin. Her rigid arm was bent at the wrist, yet there appeared to be little control of the arm motion as it occasionally fell to the side of her body. This was Allison's body, but it was not her complete being. This was a little girl who had come to join her classmates for music class and to share all the music activities that the teacher would offer during their time together.

The teacher assistant lifted Allison into a blue plastic wheelchair that was closer to the ground, so that she would not tower above her classmates. Mr. Nevan's lesson included a vocal exploration and steady beat activity at the beginning of class. "As we sing our song, what are some of the different ways that we can keep a steady beat?" The children eagerly raised their hands waiting to respond to Mr. Nevan's question. "With our hand on our other arm," suggested Jason. "Okay, with our hand. Who would like to help Allison keep a steady beat with her hand?" Again, students eagerly raised their hands, for being Allison's helper was a special responsibility that they looked forward to taking. The teacher assistant showed Jason how to move Allison's hand onto her arm, and together the entire class sang their song.

Mr. Nevan changed activities; the next song was focused on the solfège syllables "sol" and "mi." He invited each child to sing "My name is _____," while filling in the blank with her/his name. Since Allison was unable to sing her name, he asked for a volunteer to sing Allison's name into a touch recorder. This round red recorder had playback capacity whenever Allison would touch the large black area atop of the recorder. Lauren sang into the recorder. When it was Allison's turn to sing her name, the teacher assistant took Allison's fist and touched the black playback button. "My name is Al-i-son!"

Occasionally, teaching situations call for adapting teaching strategies and materials for students with needs beyond the norm. Because the authors of this text value "music education for all people," we dedicate this chapter to some of the diverse populations who might participate in music classes.

Labeling special populations is rarely satisfying or accurate. We encourage the reader to be sensitive to the fact that labels do not define a person. Each person is an individual with unique challenges and celebrations. No single label could possibly define the complexity of being human. For the purposes of this chapter, however, we will address two specific groups of "special learners" by the names with which they are typically identified: exceptional children and lifelong learners.

Every child is exceptional! Every child has individualized educational needs in a variety of domains of learning. Each child learns in a different manner and at a unique pace. Each child has educational strengths and challenges. Howard Gardner posits that every person possesses a profile of at least eight intelligences—linguistic, musical, logical-mathematical, spatial, bodily-kinesthetic, interpersonal, intrapersonal, naturalistic. Gardner's Theory of Multiple Intelligences (1983) suggests that a person's intelligence profile is not equal in strength across all intelligences. A person could be very talented in the area of music and yet not be quite as capable in the area of speaking and writing (linguistic). A person might be very social and enjoy interacting with people (interpersonal), and yet lack capabilities in drawing or painting (spatial). A person might be very intuitive and self-analytical (intrapersonal) and talented in athletic events (bodily-kinesthetic) and yet have lesser capabilities in musical talent.

What happens when a child's ability is categorized as "extreme"? What happens when a child's talent in a particular "intellectual" area exceeds that of most people? What happens when a child's performance in a particular "intellectual" area impedes her/his learning ability? These are exceptional cases that teachers encounter in their daily classroom environment. "Exceptional" is defined as "being uncommon," and "deviating wildly from the norm or average." In educational terms, being exceptional might be defined as possessing differences from the "norm" that are marked or are extreme enough to require modification or change of school services in order for the child to learn/develop.

There are many different types of exceptionalities. In the broadest of categories, exceptionalities are either physical, cognitive, behavioral, or developmental in nature. Physical exceptionalities might include students who are unable to or have limitation in their ability to walk or to move a specific appendage. They might have a disease, such as asthma, diabetes, or arthritis, which impedes their ability to participate in daily activity without accommodation. Cognitive exceptionalities include those students who score 130 or above on an IQ (intelligence quotient) test, or who have difficulty processing, organizing, or recalling information. Behavioral exceptionalities might include students who display difficulty in relationships with adults and their peers, depression, anxiety, outbursts of anger, extreme shyness, lack of control of physical behavior or verbal expression, ADD (attention deficit disorder), or ADHD (attention deficit hyperactivity disorder). Developmental delays include students who perform reading, writing, movement, and/or speech tasks at a level that is at least one grade level below the "average."

"Normal." "Average." "Learning disabled." "Gifted." What do these labels really mean? It is necessary in the educational system to label students according to their special needs and the special services that they need in order to be in a school classroom setting. Labels suggest the general characteristics of a student's disorder or disability. Labels do not, however, define who a child is. It is important to refer to a child as "having a learning disability," rather than saying that the child "is" learning disabled. The difference is that the former statement suggests that a child has a difficulty learning in one or more areas of his life skill, but that the child also possesses gifts in other areas of her/his life. The latter statement suggests that the learning disability defines the being of a child. There is so much more to a child—a human being—than that which is implied by a mere label. Students perform at the level of that which is expected of them. If they know they are labeled as "learning disabled," how might that impact their self-concept and ultimately, their self-worth?

Historical Perspective

Prior to the eighteenth century, people having disabilities or exceptionalities were typically isolated from society, because they were thought to be a creature of Satan. Popular thought had it that they were evil people whose punishment was their disability.

Compassion, increased social awareness, and understanding of the cause and effects of various exceptionalities led to the first efforts in making adaptations in materials and strategies used to educate exceptional learners. In France, during the eighteenth century, Jacob Perier and Charles Michel provided individualized instruction for people who were deaf and/or mute. There was a revision of Braille in the late eighteenth century to enable visually impaired people to read music literature. Seguin began a sensory education program during the mid-to-late 1800s. The focus was on sensation to perception, structure to creativity, known to unknown (Atterbury, 1990, pp. 4–5).

The first efforts to educate exceptional kids in the United States was at the New England Asylum for the Blind in 1832. In the twentieth century, "equal rights for all" helped bring about public awareness and sensitivity toward Americans with various disabilities. Few leaders had more devotion to eductating people with mental and physical challenges than President John F. Kennedy. His sister, Rosemary, suffered from a mental disability, an experience that made the president sensitive to others with similar difficulties. As a special needs advocate, Kennedy created councils to investigate the needs of exceptional learners and granted monetary support for research into various diseases and disabilities.

Legal Initiatives

In an attempt to recognize and to grant legal, educational, and civil rights to people with exceptional needs, Public Law (PL) 94-142 (the 142nd piece of legislation passed by the 94th United States Congress) was passed in 1975. The original law included a paragraph that required that:

> to the maximum extent appropriate, handicapped children . . . are educated with children who are not handicapped . . . and that special classes, separate schooling, or other removal of handicapped children from the regular school environment occurs only when the nature of severity of the handicap is such that education in regular classes with the use of supplementary aids and services cannot be achieved satisfactorily.

Other key principles of PL94-142 include:

- *Zero rejection*: no one can be denied education; free and appropriate education for all
- *Nondiscriminatory evaluation*: testing done according to language spoken by child and other cultural considerations; consider many aspects of child's development
- *Individualized Education Plan* (IEP): a plan that must be written for every special needs child
- *Least restrictive environment*: integration of special needs students into regular education classrooms
- *Due process:* legal procedures ensuring the rights of parents and children; professionals are held accountable for students' education; parents can hire an independent evaluator in the event that they feel the testing was biased, it has administered incorrectly, or they wish to have a second opinion
- *Parental participation*: encouraged throughout the educational planning phases

From PL94-142 came a 1990 amendment—PL101-476—that gave birth to the concept of "inclusion." Compared to the attitudes of previous centuries, the educational pendulum was now swinging to the opposite direction. Instead of isolating and refusing to educate people with disabilities, educators were now required to be fully inclusive in any educational environment, with appropriate adaptations of lesson plans or activities, use of special equipment, or help from educational specialists. PL101-476 (also known as IDEA—Individuals with Disabilities Education Act) changed the wording of PL94-142 to include all individuals with disabilities; children were not the only targeted recipients of special services. The law also focused on providing transitions from schooling to assuming responsibility at a job site. In this law, autism and traumatic brain injury were included in the list of disabilities that would be funded by the federal and state governments.

What are specific arguments for full inclusion of students in a regular classroom setting? What are the specific arguments against full inclusion? Consider the chart below. Are there other arguments to add to the list?

For Inclusion	Against Inclusion
Before laws, most exceptional students did not receive appropriate education	Schools struggle to fund educational needs of average students. Funds for special needs students takes away money from other students and educational programs.
Educate students to be a contributing member of society	Lack of teacher training, time, assistance to deal with wide variety of exceptionalities in a classroom
Free public education for all	Every student is exceptional in some way; therefore, each child should have special education plans
All students should have opportunities to learn	Exceptional children "hold back" normal and gifted children from their regular pace of learning
Schools have a responsibility to foster acceptance of people's individual differences	Costs money to test children for disabilities
Definitions used to identify people with disabilities are based on a limited measure of intellectual abilities; social biases	Exceptional students are in the minority. If one minority group receives funding, so should all minority groups within an educational setting.

Removing labels that may cause low self-esteem and underachievement

Use pull-out programs for better effectiveness, rather than fully including exceptional students with "normal" students

Exceptional students can respond at their own levels of learning

Impact on Teaching Music

Typically, exceptional students are fully included in most of the educational experiences that other students encounter throughout the school day. Special needs students, however, might receive special tutorials in a "resource room" or from another type of "pull-out" program for short periods of time throughout each day. Music is one class into which special needs students typically are "mainstreamed." That is, music class consists of students who come with varying ability levels. The music teacher is challenged to work with classroom teachers, resource room teachers, teacher assistants, parents, and other specialists in order to create a "least restrictive environment" for those students with exceptional needs, while also attending to the other children in class.

In 1986, Music Educators National Conference (MENC) released a statement concerning mainstreaming of exceptional children into regular music classes in the document, *The School Music Program: Description and Standards.* It suggests that . . .

- When handicapped students are mainstreamed into regular music classes:
  a. music educators are involved in placement decisions
  b. placement is determined primarily on the basis of musical achievement
  c. placement does not result in classes exceeding standard class size
  d. placement does not result in a disproportionate number of handicapped students in any class.
- Music instruction is provided in special education classes for those handicapped students not mainstreamed for music . . .
- Special education music classes are no larger than other special education classes, and teacher aides are provided for special education music classes if aides are provided for other special education classes (1986, pp. 25–26).

When faced with the challenge of including all students in music activities, music educators pull from their prior teaching experience, sensitivity, creativity, and knowledge of various physical, cognitive, and emotional impairments. Reliance on these characteristics help music teachers dissect expectations into small steps or actions that will help a special needs student to be successful. The first step in adapting music education is to ask questions about the specific characteristics of a student's disability and the impact the disability has on the student's ability to move, read, speak, sing, listen, see, and interact with others. Relying on assumptions that stem from a medical or educational label (i.e., "learning disabled," "gifted") might lead to inappropriate adaptations for a special needs child in the music classroom.

Recent research has suggested that music can actively access parts of the brain that speech, math, and logic processing cannot. The music classroom, then, is a place where all students might benefit from a nonverbal form of expression . . . a place that may be just what an exceptional learner needs.

CREATIVE ADAPTATIONS IN MUSIC CLASSROOM AND REHEARSALS

In this section of this chapter, we will explore special adaptations for only some of the exceptionalities that music teachers might encounter in a classroom or rehearsal setting. None of these adaptations require tremendous effort, but rather they depend on a teacher's sensitivity to all students' capabilities. One consideration is that adaptations should draw the least amount of attention to a particular student's area of special needs. The following lists of adaptations represent a compilation of ideas gleaned from Atterbury (1990) and Birkenshaw-Fleming (1993).

Adaptations for cognitive impairments

- Keep verbal instructions to a minimum.
- Use pictures to remind students of the words of a song.
- Use gross motor movement (movement of legs, arms, whole body; nothing requiring intricate coordination)
- Repeat and review throughout all lessons
- Use very fast music, if teacher wants to decrease students' uncontrollable gestures (loss of beat)
- Use rhythmic music, especially vocal music
- Choose songs with limited singing range; transposition of songs might be necessary
- Use the autoharp as an accompaniment (one person pushes buttons and the other strums)
- Use kazoos
- Use resonator bells one at a time

- Have students clap; it is easier than coordinated walking
- Sing songs with natural speech emphasis
- Use songs with an ostinato played on Orff or other classroom rhythm instruments
- Work on developing social skills (i.e., manners, sharing, taking turns)
- Work on the memory development of short rhythmic or melodic patterns

Adaptations for physical impairments

- Design flexibility warmups as attention-getters
- Use Kodály-Curwen hand signs to represent pitches and patterns
- Designate space/area for movement activities
- Develop movement sequences to recorded music
- Try wheelchair "dancing"
- Use scarf movements to a steady beat
- Throw/catch nerf balls, sponge balls
- Work on strengthening students' posture
- Sing!!! to increase breath intake
- Velcro and tape (heavy tape) instruments to lapboard or tray of wheelchair to add stability
- Include drums and hand drums since they are easy to grasp and play
- Initiate drum conversations
- Take off bars (on Orff instruments) that are not going to be used
- Color-code pitched instruments (bars)
- Use Omni chords (touch sensitive)
- Create music stand adaptations: wooden stands with drilled holes to hold instrument
- Sew jingle bells onto mittens/gloves
- Use Velcro straps to hold rattles and shakers in place
- Suspended instruments: cymbal, drum, woodblock, claves
- Glue guitar/autoharp pick to glove
- Make a finger sleeve that has pick glued to it
- Use tongue depressor as a strummer
- Make mallets larger by wrapping cloth around it (softer and easier to grip)

Adaptations for hearing impairments

- Get deaf person's attention first, then talk
- Key the person into the topic

- Speak slowly and clearly, not louder
- Look directly at person
- Do not place anything in your mouth or over your mouth (hinder student's lip-reading process)
- Maintain eye contact
- Use "I" and "You" when communicating
- Avoid standing in front of a light source (glare makes it difficult to see face without shadowing)
- Use body language in communicating
- Use open ended questions not requiring YES or NO (impaired people tend to nod yes, although they might not have a real sense of understanding)
- Use round tables instead of rows (circles if seated on floor)
- Provide new vocabulary in advance (write on chalkboard/overhead)
- Avoid pacing/unnecessary words
- Use visual aides
- Repeat questions/statements made by teacher and other students
- Use an interpreter in large group setting
- Have hearing device adjusted by the school expert for music activities
- Do not set volume of music to where the SOFTEST sounds can be heard

Adaptations for visual impairments

- Optimize students' listening skills
- Develop students' sense of mobility
- Use large-print books
- Provide magnifying devices
- Use computers to enlarge words and music of a song
- Highlight/trace lines of music with bold colored markers
- Use a reading frame to draw attention to an isolated area of a musical score
- Be careful of using too much imagery; visually impaired students might have a lag in conceptual development because of lacking experience with objects, people, places that a "normal" child has seen.
- Be certain that child understands words to the songs (ask resource teacher of child's experiences)
- Acquaint student with all areas of room (storage, location of objects). Be consistent then with how the room is arranged.
- Try Suzuki-based education (hands-on); valved instruments (one hand on valve, other on Braille)

- Speak words of affect/praise for child, rather than show facial expression or other nonverbal cue
- Say name of child then ask question
- Use contrast of printed materials: black print on yellow paper
- Use buff-colored paper, no glossy; beware of glare from laminated items
- Be certain that light source comes from behind student's shoulder
- Do not grab person's arm during movement
- Keep using "see," "look"
- Repeat melodies or rhythms so students can memorize quickly
- Send tape of melodies/words of songs home so child can memorize
- Adjust chairs/tables to bring music closer to child
- Use texture boards to represent sound/visual symbols
- Use large letters/colors/Braille embossing on instrument bars
- Velcro notes onto checkers and have them move fingers up and down on a staff
- Have students feel shapes that represent sectional forms

Adaptations for Attention Deficit Disorder (ADD)

- Use lots of visual props (objects) to hold students' attention
- Do not allow instruments/visuals to be seen until going to use them
- Use drums, since they are great attention getters. Students love to hit drums.
- Sing songs with actions
- Develop students' long-term or short-term memory
- Sing commands for a task that teacher wants students to perform
- Designate child's personal space on the floor, at a desk, in the choir/band/orchestra

Adaptations for gifted and talented

- Engage students in musical experiences that exercise their creativity—composition, performance, improvisation
- Encourage students to perform as a solo performer
- Provide private tutorials for performance, composition, improvisation
- Have a student's composition performed by a class or performance ensemble
- Use computer technology to facilitate composition
- Encourage students to conduct a research project dealing with some facet of music or history

- Provide the opportunity for students to compare recorded and/or live performances of the same piece of music
- Encourage the student to develop his/her conducting skill; conduct a piece in rehearsal and in a concert

LESSON PLAN (SEGMENT OF CLASS)

Grade level: Grade 4

Concept: Same/different (repetition/contrast)

Lesson Time: fifteen minutes

National Content Standard: 1, 2, 5

Objectives:

1. Students will imitate hand motions as they listen to "Beautiful Rain."
2. Students will hold up a shape each time they hear repetition of the initial section of "Beautiful Rain."
3. Students will sing first section of "Beautiful Rain."

Materials: CD: Ladysmith Blackmambazo, shape cutouts

Adaptations: (Hearing-impaired student)

movement, visuals, verbiage to a minimum, place items on chalkboard

Procedure:

1. Discuss how students feel about rain.

   Q: Why is rain needed? How can it be a nuisance?

2. Listen to song on CD. Teacher will do movements; students will imitate movements.
3. After listening, ask students to identify which movements were repeated throughout song.
4. Learn initial section of song with hand movements.
5. Listen again to song. Students will hold up shape whenever they hear initial section, which was just sung. Students will hold up second shape whenever they hear a differing section.

Evaluation:

ANOTHER LESSON PLAN (SEGMENT OF CLASS)

Grade: 4

Musical Concept: phrases, style

Materials: stereo system, chalkboard, music "Oh, Susanna" (World of Music, Grade 4)

Adaptations (mild/moderate visually impaired student):
  - phrase cards, dark on light, enlarged music, movement (circle movement, no partnering)

Lesson Objectives:

1. Students will trace number of phrases in song

2. Students will verbally identify same and different phrases

3. Students will describe different styles of singing the song "Oh, Susanna"

Procedure (15–20 mins.):

1. Review song, "Oh, Susanna," by rote (use music books)

2. Students "trace phrases" of song with their arm

3. Students draw symbols showing which phrases are same and which are different (melody comparison, not words)

4. Movement: circle and change direction when phrases change. Stop when phrase is different.

5. Listening segment: Direction: As we listen to the music, compare this performance of "Oh, Susanna" with the way we sang it. How is it the same? How is it different?

6. Discuss students' responses

7. Listen to performance 2. Compare with performance 1 on recording. How is performance same? Different?

8. Discuss students' responses and lead to style differences.

QUESTIONS FOR DISCUSSION

1. Identify one or two events in your life in which you were unexpectedly included in an activity. Identify one or two events in your life in which you were excluded from an activity. How did you feel? How did you react? Why?

2. In what educational or social settings have you interacted with people having physical challenges, mental challenges, emotional impairments, learning disabilities? What behaviors do you remember observing if you had interacted with special needs people?

3. How might a teacher need to adapt his/her teaching style to accommodate special needs students? How do you imagine teaching exceptional children who are included in a typical general music setting?

4. What specific challenges do performance ensemble teachers face as they attempt to fully include a special needs student in their chorus, orchestra, or band?

5. What are your ideas about how an exceptional child learns? Where did these ideas originate? Might any of these ideas be based on assumptions or stereotypes?

6. What excites you about teaching exceptional children? What are your concerns?

ASSIGNMENTS

1. Visit a general music class or a performance ensemble in which students who are identified as "special needs students" participate. As you observe the music class in action, note the following about the special learners:
   - What are the students learning about music?
   - What types of responses do you see? Does every student respond in the same manner?
   - How are these students similar to or different from those you have observed or taught?
   - How is this lesson similar to or different from other music classes you have observed or taught?
   - What specific accommodations did the teacher make so that all students were fully included into the classroom activity?

2. Case study assignment

   (Adapted from Campbell and Scott-Kassner, 1995, pp. 332–3)

Task: Determine music learning goals for each of these children in your elementary general music class. Consider their potential strengths and weaknesses. What musical, social, emotional, physical behaviors would you develop? What modifications might be necessary in your classroom?

Malinka: Age eight, loves to sing but has difficulty controlling singing voice, Down's syndrome child, moderately retarded, gift for relating joy to people around her; difficulty inhibiting responses in music class. Testing and class performance suggest that she will be able to live in a group setting and work at a job provided there as an adult.

Trevor: Age ten, active composer, replicates music by ear (plays piano by ear) but family cannot afford private piano lessons, highly gifted musically; has difficulty working in groups.

James: Age six, seeks constant attention, moves body constantly, hits children next to him, talks out of turn, rarely sings without shouting, loves to play African drums; diagnosed as having ADHD; mathematically gifted.

Veronica: Age eleven, quiet child, smiles and nods at teacher when directions are given, difficulty matching pitch, loves to play the recorder; wears two hearing aides with a receiver (teacher wears a transmitter), with hearing devices she is moderately hearing impaired.

LIFELONG LEARNING

At one of my cello lessons in high school, my private teacher asked me if I would be willing to teach an adult beginner. "How adult?" I asked. "Around seventy years old," he responded. My first reaction, thinking that this older person could not possibly be capable of much, was no. I also wondered why she wanted to begin study at this age, but I reluctantly agreed.

As I prepared for the first lesson, I realized that the usual materials for beginners were too juvenile looking, so I wrote out a few exercises and scales and tunes. When the moment arrived to meet for the lesson, I was astounded by her energy and enthusiasm for this project. During the first moments of introduction, we realized that both of us had certain apprehensions about this enterprise, but we realized quickly that we had something in common: a love of the cello.

I proceeded with the steps for basic playing posture and realized I would need to make some accommodations for her hands. They did not fall into place as young people's do and so I gently guided them in the right direction and explained the materials I had prepared. After a while I checked my watch and was shocked to realize how much time had passed and how much we had covered. Unlike most lessons with younger students, we were both so engrossed in what we were doing that we were unaware of time. We set up the next week's lesson time and I honestly looked forward to it. We both felt as though we were exploring and developing an important new chapter in our lives.

What is lifelong learning?
What population does it involve?
How does one prepare to teach older learners?
What are appropriate goals for them?
Why bother?

News reports often mention the fact that our population will be comprised of more seniors than youth when the baby boomers pass the age of sixty (U.S. Census Bureau, 1999). We are living longer and healthier than ever before. People are now looking for training and learning in new areas at all ages. "Lifelong learner" is a term developed by educators to describe older populations who are eager to be students again.

How do we as music educators fill the need of lifelong learners? Can we provide music training after public school is completed? *Vision 2020* (Madsen, 2000), a MENC publication, reports from a Gallup poll that 84 percent of the public believe that music is an important part of life, and 96 percent believe that playing a musical instrument provides lifelong enjoyment. Transition is key to successful lifelong musical participation, meaning that while students are still in school, they should make connections with the community musical organizations that will be available after they graduate.

A special focus issue of the *Music Educator's Journal* (December 1992) is dedicated to the topic of lifelong learning. One article by Jacquelyn Boswell (1992) describes human needs as being threefold: identity, partnership, and participation. Music can satisfy each of these needs. In *Meaning-Making: Therapeutic Processes in Adult Development* by Carlsen (1988), it was proposed that music can bring meaning to our lives through identification with particular styles of music and the cultures from which they come. Because we experience music in partnership and participation with other people through singing or instrument playing, music activities can be especially valuable to the lifelong learner. Community centers cater to music-makers of all ages. Elderhostels are one notable example of this phenomenon. As learners, adults may be more likely than children to recognize their need for learning and to pursue it voluntarily.

Reasons for Beginning Music Instruction as an Adult/Senior

Many people regret having stopped lessons as a child or not having had the opportunity to study music or take private lessons. As adults, people often have the time, the resources, and the personal incentive to follow a dream. Many times, there is a desire to play familiar tunes, hymns, and songs as they reflect on their lives and memories. Such reflection brings a richness to adults' current time and an affirmation of the past. Leisure time is filled and quality of life is enhanced through the communication and social contact that music entails. Additionally, emotions expressed through music can aid in relieving depression, and music activities can help organize time and encourage exercise.

Characteristics of the Adult/Senior Learner

Adult/senior learners are often willing and eager to work. Typically, they have very clear goals, the ability to stay on task, advanced analytical and theoretical thinking, and concern with process more than the end product. Adult experiences have brought them to this point, and gratitude and intrinsic motivation are high.

Difficulties for Adult/Seniors in Pursuing Their Desires

Many lifelong learners have doubts that they are capable of learning a new skill. The possibility of physical and emotional challenges are important for the teacher to acknowledge.

- Physical limitations can affect skills like dexterity
- Sight, hearing, and short-term memory may be waning
- Past musical experiences may have been unsuccessful
- Beginning materials are usually geared for young people
- Health may interfere with seniors' ability to be regular in their participation
- Feelings of inadequacy may cause reluctance or inconsistency in attendance

What can be done to guide seniors past these difficulties? The answer is similar to that of any teaching situation: Adapt expectations and activities so that students can be successful. Starting from the known and working toward the unknown, and using tunes that are familiar to that group of people are quite effective. Different cultures may have a preference for certain types of music. The pace may need to be slower than with younger students, and some material may need to be printed larger. Keep in mind also that activities will need to vary so muscles do not get stiff or tired.

Opportunities We Can Offer

Many colleges offer programs for participation in the arts by community members. One organization that has established weeklong seminars on campuses is Elderhostel. This organization began in 1975 with age as the only requirement for participation (60+). Elderhostel involves colleges, universities, and other educational institutions with a variety of course offerings. Programs are usually one week in length and include field trips, sight-seeing, no credit, and no exams. Examples for senior groups include hand-bell playing in Georgia, recorder playing in Kansas, clog dancing and dulcimer making in North Carolina, musical theater study in Idaho, Gospel Choir singing in California, and colonial dancing in Williamsburg, Virginia. Participants come from many walks of life: a surgeon taking piano lessons, a secretary taking part in dance contests, and an engineer who makes instruments. A quarter of a million people participate in these courses yearly all over the world.

Group rather than individual instruction tends to be more successful with adults/seniors. In the group they do not feel alone in their challenges, and they enjoy the camaraderie of others seeking new skills and information. Ensemble music is often more satisfactory than playing a solo. An interestingly popular idea is group keyboard labs. These electronic labs offer an immense variety of sounds. The electronic keyboards are also an advantage in their capability for soundproof practice that does not disturb others, thanks to headphones.

For seniors, ensemble opportunities in choirs, bands, and orchestras, as well as church choirs, may hold exciting possibilities. Some of these ensembles are cropping up all over the United States in senior centers and community centers.

Ensembles can also provide an opportunity for intergenerational experiences. Younger people may not be aware of the daily lives of adults/seniors. David Frego (1995) reports on a program in Canada called Interlink, which was started to overcome intergenerational stereotypes. A musical director contacted a school and an adult institution and requested volunteers to participate as a writing partner and then to join in a choir. Seniors were asked to respond to the youths' letters within a week, and a flow of communication was established. The musical director rehearses the youth and adults at their own institutions on the same music carefully selected for the voices. After a few weeks, there is a joint rehearsal. The participants were eager to meet their pen-pals and then to join in singing and a shared meal. This innovative program has grown to include many different communities in Canada.

Eastman School of Music started a New Horizons Band for beginning players in the Rochester area. The only requirement was that a person had to be over fifty years of age. The turnout was terrific, and the group was very proud of their progress in the year. Many other bands for seniors now exist across the United States.

Recommendations for senior programs

- Select materials that appeal to adults
- Encourage intergenerational ensemble participation
- Consider ways to incorporate newer technology (electronic keyboards, etc.)
- Locate the adult learning center central to public transportation
- Offer flexible membership requirements
- Document what works and share it with other music educators
- Replicate curricular offerings among performing, listening, and creating activities

The current population of older adults is more educated than past generations of seniors. Many are musically literate, enthusiastic, sensitive, and able and willing to make music. The reward is substantial, the effort worthwhile to share time and music with them.

SAMPLE LESSON FOR AN INTERGENERATIONAL CHOIR

Objective: To be able to sing together joyously.

Materials: "Ching a Ring Chaw," Copland
       "A River Runs Wide"

Warmup: backrubs, stretches, voice swoops, consonant patterns (do-be . . .)

Ching a Ring Chaw: say the words slowly and crisply

       sing the tune on du
       sing bass-line on du
       sing own part with words at moderate tempo

Break

A River Runs Wide: sing legato interval leaps to gain vocal control
       sing the tune on du and have your hand make an arch in the air
         for each phrase
       add the words
       add dynamics

This lesson plan is a basic sketch of what could be covered in a half-hour choir rehearsal. The repertoire is American, light-hearted, and accessible technically. Be sure to move through it at a relaxed, but flowing pace. People do not appreciate being "stuck" in one part of a song for long.

QUESTIONS FOR DISCUSSION

1. What is lifelong music learning? Why should it be valued?
2. What are characteristics of an adult/senior learner?
3. What challenges to learning might the teacher/conductor need to address when dealing with adult/senior learners?

4. What opportunities for adults/seniors exist? What can be developed in your hometown?

5. If more seniors are involved in music making, what implications can it have for our children?

REFERENCES

Exceptional learners

CAMPBELL, P. and SCOTT-KASSNER, C. (1995). *Music in Childhood*. New York: Simon and Schuster Macmillan.

GARDNER, H. (1983). *Frames of Mind: The Theory of Multiple Intelligences*. New York: Basic Books.

MADSEN, C., ed. (2000). *Vision 2020*. Reston, VA: MENC.

Music Educators National Conference (MENC). (1986). *The School Music Program: Description and Standards*. Reston, VA: MENC.

Lifelong learning

BOSWELL, J. (December 1992). "Human Potential and Lifelong Learning." *Music Educators Journal* 79(4), pp. 38–40.

BIRKENSHAW-FLEMING, L. (1993). *Music for All: Teaching Music to People with Special Needs*. Toronto, ON: Thompson Music.

CARLSON, M. (1988). *Meaning-Making: Therapeutic Processes in Adult Development*. New York: Norton.

FREGO, D. (May 1995). "Uniting the Generations with Music Programs." *Music Educators Journal* 81(6), pp. 17–19, 55.

MADSEN, C. (ed.). (2000). *Vision 2020: The Housewright Symposium on the Future of Music Education*. Reston, VA: MENC.

MUSIC EDUCATORS NATIONAL CONFERENCE (MENC). (December 1992). *Special Focus Issue: Special Learners* 79(4).

Valuable Resources (Exceptional learners)

ATTERBURY, B. (1990). *Mainstreaming Exceptional Learners in Music*. Englewood Cliffs, NJ: Prentice Hall.

BIRKENSHAW-FLEMING, L. (1993). *Music for All: Teaching Music to People with Special Needs*. Toronto, ON: Thompson Music.

SCHABERG, G. (ed.). (1988). *Tips: Teaching Music to Special Learners*. Reston, VA: MENC.

TUTTLE, F., BECKER, L., and SOUSA, J. (1993). *Characteristics and Identification of Gifted and Talented Students*. Washington, DC: National Education Association.

Professional Associations

American Music Therapy Association
8455 Colesville Road, Suite 1000
Silver Springs, MD 20910
301-589-3300
<http://www.musictherapy.org>

Music Educators National Conference (MENC)
The National Association for Music Education
1806 Robert Fulton Drive
Reston, VA 20191
800-336-3768
<http://www.menc.org>

Other Valuable Internet Resources
(Exceptional learners)

New York Institute for Special Education
999 Pelham Parkway
Bronx, NY 10469
718-519-7000
<http://www.nyise.spec.ed>

Legal issues, special education definitions, resources, teaching assistance
<http://reedmartin.com>

11

Special Topics

I walked into a high school band rehearsal at 1:00 P.M. to watch my former director teach the ensemble. I was surprised by how unruly the students seemed to be before the rehearsal, but I was impressed by how Ms. Smith settled the class. I realized that the class was set up in a normal rehearsal setting and that the order of the rehearsal was listed on the chalkboard. The bulletin boards held various bits of music symbols and information about upcoming events and college auditions.

Ms. Smith raised her hand, the class gradually turned its attention to her, and the warmup period began. The sounds began to blend and form a pleasant ensemble. The players then launched into the first piece with great gusto. During the pauses, Ms. Smith's comments were gentle and encouraging. Sometimes she sang a part or slowed the tempo to clean up a section of music that was particularly challenging. At times, she shouted over the ensemble, "Nice!," or "Good!," or other words of encouragement and praise. The players responded positively. Some players were talking in the back of the ensemble, but softly enough to not interfere with others. At one stopping point, Ms. Smith waited a while to make sure all were quiet before she continued the rehearsal. Overall, a lot was accomplished.

This chapter will deal with three areas that are often of special interest to students—classroom management, technology, and career options with a music education degree.

CLASSROOM MANAGEMENT

Most undergraduate music education majors are eager to learn as much as they can about classroom management. And most preservice teachers will say that the aspect of teaching that worries them most is managing discipline in their classrooms. Although the topic of classroom management is clearly an important one to cover in teacher preparation courses, training music education majors in classroom management skills is nearly impossible. Teaching classroom management outside the context of a classroom is a little like training the defensive team in football with no offensive players to oppose them. It is one thing to talk about how to handle classroom situations, but with no students to run interference, it is all academic—literally.

According to Single (1991), research has revealed several effective strategies for classroom management in music classes. Well-constructed lessons with explicit instructions, systematic integration of rules and procedures, and the well-known teaching sequence of demonstration-wait time-guided practice-assessment are all ways in which attention and focus can be maximized in the classroom. In addition, Single found the following to be "best practices" as suggested by music teacher-experts:

quick pacing
appropriate vocal modeling
competent conducting gestures
appropriate approval
good eye contact
varied physical proximity
clear directions
pleasant affect
musical conviction
confident/in control appearance
on-task students
good voice
good personality
good questions
positive approach
enthusiastic affect

Classroom Management Tips

Classroom management has many influences, including the classroom environment itself, the school, and the home. Because excellent classroom management is tied closely with excellent teaching, teachers should provide an environment that is conducive to learning—one that encourages and reinforces students to stay focused. The following list of practical reminders may be helpful.

The Classroom Environment

- arrange classroom for easy "flow"
- arrange in a way so as to see all students easily and so that all students can see you
- arrange in a way so that you can move throughout room easily (around and in between chairs, etc.)
- check students' seating arrangements frequently to help students stay focused
- classroom rules/expectations and consequences, both positive and negative, are posted clearly

The Teacher

- eye contact
- enthusiasm—students stay on task more when they know teacher is excited about what he/she is teaching
- know your material
- be able to adapt "on the spot" if needed
- use lots of positive reinforcement for desired behaviors: smile, praise, incentives, and so on
- use extrinsic motivators, if needed, to help students develop INTRINSIC motivation to achieve and stay on task
- proximity—use throughout lesson, but especially when you notice off-task behavior; move toward student but keep your lesson flowing
- plan interesting lessons with lots of participation and involvement
- be fair and consistent
- when a rule has been broken and negative consequences occur, emphasize the child's BEHAVIOR rather than the child himself or herself—each day is a fresh start
- minimize transitions
- use cues and signals effectively
- be conscious of lesson/rehearsal pacing

The School Environment

- should support all teachers' classroom management; there is also a school-wide discipline plan in place that is constantly reinforced by all teachers and administrators

The Home Environment

- parents are aware of all classroom rules/expectations and are kept informed of child's behavior, "good" as well as "bad"
- parents' support is solicited; parents are involved in classroom activities, concerts, and other events

In a Rehearsal

- be organized—start rehearsal on time
- rehearse efficiently—keep them busy
- project your voice
- keep an eye on percussion section
- spend more time rehearsing than talking
- keep eye contact with all sections

- know names
- watch pacing, do not rehearse one section too long
- teach the ensemble to stop playing immediately when you stop
- place the order of rehearsal on blackboard or outside room
- chair and stands should be in place before rehearsal begins
- use humor at times to ease tension
- end rehearsals on time
- each student should have a pencil
- get off podium and walk around the group and stop conducting

Preventive Medicine on the Part of the Teacher

- learn students' names
- consistency of rule enforcement
- students' knowledge of rules (school and class): student contract of behavior
- realizing student behaviors not same as adults
- identify your own tolerance level, recognizing will vary per day/change over time
- have planned consequences that match the behavior
- respond early
- use verbal and nonverbal interaction
- one-on-one discussion (especially older children): not to embarrass in front of peers
- be certain to tell students of the behavior, not the person behind the behavior, that is inappropriate
- be certain that the student is aware of the *specific* behavior that is inappropriate
- do not let the situation disrupt the learning of others or the flow of instruction
- do not let the situation turn into a power struggle; if anger ensues, you have waited too long to deal with the situation
- student Age = number of minutes per activity: VARIETY
- planning
- challenging, but not unattainable activities in class
- interactive, interesting
- pacing
- creativity
- know the context and prepare to avoid situations—know your students as individuals; be prepared to change the context in which potential misbehavior might occur

Helpful Hints

Rules

- never more than five
- observable
- consistent
- specific

Other Tips

- never expect behavior you have not taught
- practice running all equipment before using it
- go over the plan
- consider giving choices of activities rather than free time
- write assignments, repeat often
- study class rosters—check pronunciations
- reseat seasoned students after they choose seats
- be polite and respectful
- dismiss class yourself
- protect privacy of your space (desk)
- stay on your feet and move around
- coach rather than criticize
- return contraband if appropriate to do so (after first consulting school policy)
- refrain from touching students
- send to office whenever absolutely necessary and appropriate
- know school and district policies
- do not keep fund-raising money; give to secretary
- maintain accurate records, grades, and document conversations
- do not show favoritism
- get to know the office personnel
- if you go to the faculty room, do not add to gossip
- do not discuss student in another's presence
- know that you'll make mistakes; the sun still rises
- problems are likely to occur during free time, transitions, interruptions

Assignment

In your field work, choose one student to observe each visit and make notes on her/his behavior and how the teacher responds. Write a reaction each time as to how you might have handled the situation differently from the way the teacher did. Consider the behavior from the viewpoint of the student and of the teacher.

TECHNOLOGY

Technology has a new dimension these days beyond the record player and movie projector of the last century. We are now faced with a constantly developing field of options in technological support for our teaching. Many teachers have access to and use the most recent technological equipment in their classrooms. Other teachers may not consider themselves to be on the "cutting edge" of technological knowledge and use in their music classrooms. It is impossible to prepare teachers for what the future of technology might hold. An attitude of flexibility is important for teachers to be open to possibilities that are available to them in their situations. Let's examine some basic requirements.

Sound Reproduction

Listening experiences are crucial for a music class. The basic equipment for listening is a compact disc player as a part of a complete high-quality stereo system. A remote control frees the teacher to stop and start the CD from any position in the room.

Presentation Products

The most basic display format is the chalkboard or dry-erase board, which allows many students to do their work where the class can see what they are doing. Overhead projectors are also convenient to enlarge prepared documents. Video players and televisions are standard equipment for presenting videos and documentaries in classrooms. Teachers can prepare HyperCard presentations and use PowerPoint or other computer-based programs to have specially prepared visual and audio instruction simultaneously. At this point, these products require substantial knowledge, experience, and preparation time.

Hands-On Computer Terminals

Students are now able to access computer programs through sequencers, midi, and digital cameras so that they can write their own music and make their own films. Programs also exist for students to play "games" that teach about music notation and symbols. Some programs include audio playback to develop students' listening skills. Software to notate music allows students to print their music with professional appearance.

Listing specific software programs currently available for use would likely be outdated as soon as this book is published. We advise teachers to check with a music store or to attend computer workshops at conferences or colleges to update themselves on the newest innovations that could enhance their teaching.

Assignment: Music Education Software

Goal: To review and critique samples of music education software that are available for classroom/ensemble use

Objective: Students will be able to use a software program as a tool in their instruction of a class

A. Peruse software programs contained in the "Music Education Folder" in the computer lab
   1. Practica Musica
   2. Pitch Explorer
   3. Keyboard Kapers
   4. Adventures in Musicland
   5. Music Ace
   6. Listen
   7. MusicShop, Finale, Sibelius
   8. Rock, Rap, and Roll
   9. Making Music, Making More Music
   10. Band in a Box
   11. Guitar Made Easy
   12. The PowerPoint Portfolio Builder
   13. HyperStudio
B. Select one program that you want to explore thoroughly

C. After exploring the program, write a two-page, word-processed review of its content, providing a critique of its activities and content and speculating how you might incorporate the program in a general music class or performance ensemble setting

D. In your review and critique, address the following questions:

1. Is the program designed as computer-assisted instructional software (drill and practice) or composing and creative music making software?

2. What music skill or knowledge does the software reinforce?

3. How specifically might you incorporate this software program into a music education setting? In which grades would you use this program? What type of class? When, during your music class, would you have students working with the program? Support your responses with rationale.

4. What are the unique/exciting features of the program that students would find appealing?

5. What might give students difficulty as they use the program? What glitches, if any, did you notice? How would you, the teacher, prepare students for this in order to avoid potential student frustration?

6. You are a music teacher with a specified budget. Would you purchase this piece of software for use in your school? Why or why not?

Evaluation criteria: Papers will receive a letter grade based on content (creativity, application of ideas, completeness) and writing style (grammar, spelling, format).

CAREER OPTIONS IN MUSIC EDUCATION

A person with a music education degree can take several different avenues and turns in her/his career. The degree is preparation for many different options. The obvious career is that of a PreK–12 music teacher. Many wonderful opportunities abound in that arena. Parallel to the public school music teacher is a private school music teacher. Private schools and other alternative schools are abundant, and a person with a particular philosophical or religious viewpoint might be more comfortable in some of these situations. Another level of teaching is college or higher education, requiring graduate degrees in order to pursue these positions. For higher education positions, the undergraduate and graduate degrees may be combinations of music performance and music education, but music education faculty positions usually require some public school experience.

Private instruction may be an avocation or may be a primary source of income for a musician. If one's degree is in music education, the teacher's understanding of the learning process for the student is more broad, because of many field experiences and educational psychology courses.

Some musicians with a music education degree go on to performance careers, music administrative careers, community music school positions, or work in the music retail field. Undergraduate music school is the time to explore the many avenues and keep options open for the possibilities that may arise and to best use one's talents.

REFERENCES

BARTLEBAUGH, K., THOMAN, K., and WEBER, H. (1996). *The Focused Classroom: Decoding Student Behavior, Grade K–6.* Berkeley, CA: Spectrum Center.

FUNG, V. (May–June 2000). "The Internet: A Connection to World Musics." *Triad* 67(8), pp. 33–4.

MADSEN, C., STANDLEY, J., BYO, J., and CASSIDY, J. (1991). "Assessment of Effective Teaching by Instrumental Music Student Teachers and Experts." *Update: Research Applications in Music Teaching,* 10(1), p. 20.

SINGLE, N. (1991). "A Summary of Research-Based Principles of Effective Teaching." *Update: Research Applications in Music Teaching,* 9(2), p. 3.

WEBSTER, P. (1995). "General Music, School Reform, and Technology." In S. Stauffer (ed.), *Toward Tomorrow: New Visions for General Music.* Reston, VA: MENC.

WIGGINS, J. (1990). *Composition in the Classroom: A Tool for Teaching.* Reston, VA: MENC.

WIGGINS, J. (1995). "Where does Technology Belong in the General Music Curriculum?" In Stauffer, S. (ed.), *Toward Tomorrow: New Visions for General Music.* Reston, VA: MENC.

WIGGINS, J. (1991). *Synthesizers in the Elementary Classroom: An Integrated Approach.* Reston, VA: MENC.

WIGGINS, J. (2001). *Teaching for Musical Understanding.* New York: McGraw-Hill.

WILLIAMS, D. and WEBSTER, P. (1996). *Experiencing Music Technology: Software, Data, and Hardware.* New York: Schirmer.

12

Developing a Philosophy of Music Education

First-year teacher Ms. Haskins has just taken a job as string specialist in a large school district in an urban community. The parents of students in the school district met last winter and spring with the school district's administrative team, and together they decided that there was enough interest in string music education to start a program in the school district in the fall.

Knowing that the task of starting a string program from the "ground up" would be an overwhelming, yet not impossible, task, Ms. Haskins began to think about what she wanted the ultimate string program to resemble. She realized that in the initial stages of building the program, the "ultimate" would not occur immediately, but she thought it productive to have program goals in mind for the future. Ms. Haskins dreamt about wonderful solo and orchestral performances, students playing in tune, musically satisfied students, parents, and administrators. She would begin with the youngest students and build the program through the high school level.

Then, it occurred to her! She had been imagining only one of the "end products" of string music education—staging quality performances. But how was she going to achieve her end results? Wanting her program to be a viable music program, she began to design a curriculum. She was confronted with having to determine what was musically appropriate for her students to learn. When were they to learn the various skills and musical knowledge necessary to become an independent musician? Why did the school district and the community want a string program? What were their goals and motives? Did they coincide with hers? Why did she value string music education?

Ms. Haskins's simple dream unleashed a host of provocative questions, the answers to which would determine what was taught, when it was taught, why it was taught, and how it was taught. Her head began to spin when she realized that she had to take a personal look inward; she needed to reflect on and sort through these vital issues that would drive her curriculum and ultimately would determine the success of her string program.

Where would she begin? She felt quite confident in the amount of knowledge and performance experience she had acquired throughout her years of formal string training. Inwardly, she knew why string music education was important, but she was unable to articulate her thoughts and feelings. She read articles and portions of books that discussed curricular ideas, some with which she agreed and others that did not seem natural to her. She consulted other music educators for ideas. One older band director who had taught for many years finally said to her, "Look, in the end it comes down to what you believe is important. What do you value—not only about a school having a string program—but why are you convinced that music education is a valuable part of every student's basic education? What is your philosophy, your rationale? You need a foundation on which to build your program. You will make your decision, parts of which may or may not coincide with what some other music education professionals deem important." Ms. Haskins had a lot of thinking and soul-searching to do over the remaining portion of the summer, before her first string students eagerly arrived during the first week of school in September.

INTRODUCTION

Some music educators would contend that a chapter on developing a philosophy of music education should be the initial chapter in a book that introduces undergraduates to the music education profession. The authors of this book, however, believe that one's personal philosophy of music education is a continuously evolving journey taken during one's professional life. Through this journey, a philosophy motivates a teacher's instructional style and course content and is redesigned or confirmed by practical teaching experience. A reciprocal process, developing a philosophy of teaching is a continuous challenge, something that should not be allowed to become dormant or stagnant. Therefore, we are relying on the probability that your teaching observations, teaching episodes, and class readings and discussions during this semester have informed and expanded the conception of the music education profession that you first brought to this class.

There is no single, widely accepted philosophy of music education—a problem and a plus for our music education profession. First, having no uniform philosophy of teaching is a problem; the music teaching profession might be strengthened if its teachers could agree on what should be taught to students and why music education should exist for all students. The creation of the *National Standards for Arts Education* (MENC, 1994) was an attempt to unify individuals' concepts of curricular content across age levels. The lack of a standardized philosophy is a plus, however, because each teacher is empowered to make personal decisions based on personal values. Every time a music educator makes a decision that affects who, what, why, when, or how she/he teaches, values are exhibited and set into motion. The authors of this text made conscious decisions of why, when, and for whom we were writing this book, as well as what content we would present and how we would present it. Each chapter reflects values of individual authors and the writing team as a unified entity. We chose to include and present the content in a certain fashion according to our teaching experience in the public schools and according to our personal philosophies of music education.

This chapter will include bits of historical perspective including some of the social, political, and cultural events that influenced the existence of formalized music education in American society. In your advanced music education courses, you will acquire additional depth and breadth of historical and philosophical perspective as it relates to music education. Therefore, the authors will present only some of the significant historical events, prominent thinkers, and general philosophical ideas from which many music educators draw their passions about teaching.

Many questions will be posed in this chapter. Few, if any, definitive answers will be provided. The purpose of this chapter, however, is to stimulate your thinking about why you are considering music education as a profession, why you deeply believe that music is important to humans, and why children of all ages should experience music education. If you were asked to articulate why you value music as an art or why you are committed to the music education profession, could you state your views and values? Could you justify your opinions? Read and consider the following ideas presented in this chapter with an open mind. It is the authors' intent that the structure of this chapter will facilitate the development of a brief philosophy statement of music education, one that you might choose to rework, reword, redefine, and redo throughout your music education journey in college and in the profession.

EXAMINING VALUES

Fundamental in formulating a philosophical statement that, with preservice and professional teaching experience and learned information, will blossom into a personal philosophy of music education is the identification of your personal values and passions regarding music and music education. In order to begin the process of writing a brief philosophical statement about music education, ask yourself, "What do I value about music?" and "What do I value about music education?" Jot down your ideas, save them, and build on them as you consider the ideas presented in this chapter. The chart that follows might assist you in organizing your thoughts. In each box, place a word or phrase that indicates how music education plays a uniquely important role in developing that feature of human beings. The chart already has an entry in each category in order to provide an example of the many extant possibilities.

"Why do I value music and/or music education?"

Intellectual	Emotional	Physical and/ or Behavioral	Personality	Social	Other
Learn to read a different symbol system	Means of expression	Muscle coordination in singing and playing instruments	Builds self-confidence	Learn to work within a group	Exercises the "ears" (sensory stimulation)

You probably have automatic responses to the "why" questions, for you have been drawn into exploring the music education profession because you love music. You understand at the deepest human level what it is like to experience music and the joys that performing, listening, composing, and improvising music have brought to your life over the past years. You probably want to share your passion for music with your future music students. But, this passion is not the only justification for creating and maintaining quality music education programs.

Before you set aside your list, review the values and passions contained in each column of your list. Most, if not all, values tend to fall into two broad categories—musical reasons for valuing music education and extramusical reasons for valuing music education. Musical reasons for having music education programs focus on music as a unique art form and learning about the various components making a complete piece of music. Extramusical reasons, while important, are reasons not having to do with the music itself, but are ancillary benefits that students receive from participating in a school's music program. Extramusical reasons, sometimes referred to as "nonmusical" reasons for valuing music education, include the development of personal, social, humanistic traits that are often a result of participating in musical experiences.

You have just considered some of the "why" questions about music and music education. Try taking your ideas from the previous chart and transferring them to the following chart that indicates musical and extramusical values of music and/or music education. You might find it easier to complete this chart than the previous one, because the categories are broader and less confining. Feel free to continue brainstorming about your values, experiences, and passions, while adding your ideas to this chart.

Musical Reasons	Extramusical Reasons
Understand the creation process of a musical art form	Bolster students' self-esteem
Discriminating quality in performance with regard to expressive line	Students learn to work as a group
Participating in composition by small groups	Enjoyment

As you continue your path in music education, observe music classes, and begin practice teaching, you will gain ideas and information to add to your list of values and experiences. As you explore the music education profession, you will also want to consider pertinent "who," "what," "where," "when," and "how" questions. This list includes only a few of the most important questions to consider.

WHO?

- Who should receive music education?
- Should all students, regardless of musical ability, experience music education?
- Who should teach music education?

WHAT?

- What specific music experiences should students encounter?
- What should students learn about music?
- What musical behaviors should students exhibit during and after instruction?
- What musics should students encounter?

WHERE?

- Where should music education occur?
- In what educational setting should music education occur?
- Where, outside of schools, might music education occur?

WHEN?

- When should students learn specific music information?
- When should students have specific musical experiences?
- When should music education begin?

HOW?

- How should music education be taught?
- How might the music content standards inform teachers' decisions for curricular content?

Asking the questions, "who," "what," "where," "when," "how," and "why" in regards to education, in the broadest sense, and music education, more specifically, is not a recent phenomenon. Writings about educational policy and procedure date back to the times of great thinkers such as Plato, Aristotle, Socrates, and Erasmus. They, too, grappled with the notion of how education could best meet the functional and moral needs of a democratic society. Although times and people have changed through the millennia, some of the same basic philosophical questions that the great thinkers asked are still being posed and debated by contemporary scholars. A list of questions considered by ancient and twentieth-/twenty-first-century scholars (John Dewey, Maxine Greene, Paulo Freire, Cornel West, and Matthew Lipman, among others) includes:

- What is the role of education in a free and just society?
- What is the relationship between school and other sources of learning?
- What is the relationship between knowing and doing?
- What determines "ability"—nature or nurture?
- How does education affect people's abilities to rise above oppression?
- How does one build a learning partnership between student and teacher?
- How is a child-centered learning environment created?

Although these questions relate to complex issues surrounding education in the broadest sense, they also directly relate to music education. Substitute "music education" whenever the questions refer to "education."

How does this change the meaning of the question? Think of how your past general education and music education experiences shape your responses to those questions. Perhaps you have not had experiences that contribute to formulating a response or an opinion for a particular question. Challenge yourself to imagine placing yourself in a situation different from the one you experienced during your school years. Once again, you will have experiences in your future music education and general education courses that will help you open your mind to these questions and diverse music learning situations.

CONSIDERING THE "MOVERS AND SHAKERS"

There are select people and historical events that have shaped American music education as it exists today. Why might it be important to consider these events and various thinkers' perspectives as one attempts to formulate a statement of music education philosophy? A valuable exercise might be to try to detect hints of your own music education perspective in those people who have traveled before you in their music education journey. How did a particular individual display her/his values? How did a belief system shape the means by which music education was conducted, the people who received music education, or the musical content that was conveyed to students? Values are the foundation for action taken.

Music for Religious Purpose

In Chapter 8, you read about the European settlers who came to the North American continent in order to acquire religious and financial freedom. On their arrival, the settlers encountered indigenous American people, whose musics and societal traditions were different from the European traditions. Instead of integrating the cultural heritages, the European settlers attempted to enculturate the North American natives across the vast continent.

Music was seen as having utilitarian purposes. That is, music served the settlers in teaching their kin and the native peoples about Christian religious tradition. Bringing the Ainsworth version of psalmody from England, the Puritans published *The Bay Psalm Book* (Day, 1640). There remained limited congregational singing, however, for most common people had no training in reading musical notation or in producing quality vocal sound. Church schools were the site not only for religious education but also for teaching students hymns and psalms that would serve as core leadership within Sunday worship services.

Music in the Community

Eventually, community members, outside of the church school auspices, assumed responsibility for musically educating people. The first singing school opened in Boston (1717) with the intent of teaching music reading and cultivating singing that was more pleasing to the ear than typical congregational singing. In addition to the singing schools, Samuel Holyoke (1806) opened a school for teaching instrumental music.

The primary purpose of singing schools was to develop citizens' music notation-reading skills and to prepare those people with exceptional musical talent to sing with singing societies. New England was the host for the first singing societies, which focused on the community performance aspect of music. Their performances were not limited to performance in church worship services, but they were always inclusive of literature, which modern-day musicians might term as "the great choral masterworks."

Music for Every Child

Lowell Mason might be considered the father of modern music education. He claimed that every child deserved to learn music as a part of her/his daily school curriculum. In 1838, he became the first supervisor of elementary school vocal music, as well as the first music teacher in the Boston public schools. Mason's idea was reiterated in 1919 by Osbourne McConathy, who stated that "every child should be educated in music education according to his natural capacities" and by Karl Gehrkens who, in 1923, claimed his goal of having "music for every child, every child for music" (Abeles, Hoffer, and Klotman, 1994, p. 35).

The post–Civil War and World War I eras left music education in demand throughout the United States, particularly with a renewed interest in instrumental music. Therefore, more music educators were trained and supervised in public and private school settings. In 1907, music supervisors who were also members of the National Education Association (NEA) met for their first meeting in Keokuk, Iowa. The group assumed the name "Music Supervisors National Conference," then "Music Educators Exhibitors Association," "Music Supervisors National Conference," and, finally, "Music Educators National Conference" (Abeles, Hoffer, and Klotman, 1994, p. 36). MENC, the name it presently touts, is the music education profession's largest and most politically active group of music educators. MENC recognizes basic professional values of and standards for music education and is a strong advocate of "music for every child."

Back to Basics

During the 1950s, the United States government was prompted to invest monies into the educational system, because its chief competitor—the former Soviet Union—had just launched Sputnik. From the government's perspective, Americans would not fall behind the Soviets in the technological space race. Therefore, school reform was necessary; the "basics"—reading, math, and science—received much financial and educational attention. Many music educators would claim that the "back to basics" movement took away from music programs within the public schools.

As a reactionary attempt to regain the stature of music education among other core curricular domains, music experts met at the Yale Seminar in 1963 and at the Tanglewood Symposium in 1967. During the Yale Seminar, music experts explored means for focusing on the arts in public schools. They also examined why K–12 public school music students were not becoming musically literate. The Yale Seminar delegates concluded that music students should be exposed to a variety of musical exemplars, rather than the limited "school music" that often decontextualized the musical experience from "real life." Included in their suggestions for music education was for students to experience musics from outside of the Western musical tradition. This suggestion came as the United States was awakening to the notion of civil rights and multiculturalism.

The music historian Michael Mark (2000) stated that yet another professional gathering comprised of the music education profession's own professional and scholarly personnel was needed. The Tanglewood Symposium occurred at the summer residence of the Boston Symphony Orchestra in 1967. During the Tanglewood Symposium, music education professionals considered the effects on music education of school reform, civil rights, multicultural music issues, and the emerging role of technology. Both the Yale Seminar and the Tanglewood Symposium held as its primary objective not only to evaluate music methods and materials but also to move the profession toward creating a unified philosophy of music education.

Music for Music's Sake

Unlike the early North American settlers who considered music as a tool to promote religious doctrine, some arts education scholars of the twentieth century contemplated the value of experiencing music for music's sake. That is, music as an art form needs no utilitarian reason for being experienced by all people.

A branch of philosophy that deals with the intrinsic value of art—in this case, music as a unique art form—is called aesthetics. Experts in the field of aesthetics ponder questions such as, "What is art?," "What is the value of art in society?," and "To what aspects of art do people relate that might evoke an emotional response?" Music education as aesthetic education calls for students to learn to perceive and respond to the value of music that they listen to and perform. Three basic schools of thought represent what is important to learn and experience in an artwork.

Formalists would posit that musical elements—rhythm, form, melody, duration, dynamics, timbre, harmony—and how they interact within a musical work are of primary importance in valuing a piece of music. References and associations to the outside world (including mentally created pictures and images) are not of primary importance to one who embraces the formalist view.

Referentialists, by contrast, find meaning and value of a piece of music in its outside context, culture, and association with the real world. The referentialist point of view purports that a piece of music refers to something separate from the musical elements. A musical work and its interacting sounds function to remind the listener of something from their own life experience, from the composer's life experience, from a cultural event, or from a story.

Finally, absolute expressionists would contend that music's worth is found in the inner workings of the musical elements and that cultural experiences and context are also important in giving personal cognitive—perceptual and emotional (affective)—meaning to those inner elemental interactions. Absolute expressionism considers multiple facets of the music experience and combines them to make meaning a holistic experience of the complete piece of music.

In his landmark publication, *A Philosophy of Music Education*, Bennett Reimer (1970, 1989) provided the music education profession with a model music education philosophy. Reimer embraces the absolute expressionist philosophy, providing teachers with a rationale for creating comprehensive music curricula in performance and general music classes. His philosophy (music education as aesthetic education) remained the accepted music education philosophy, virtually unchallenged by other documented philosophies until the 1990s. Reimer suggested that aesthetic music experience involves the mind (cognition, perception) and the emotions (affective response) and that aesthetic experience can occur in a variety of musical experiences provided to students in music instruction.

Estelle Jorgensen, at Indiana University, in 1990 organized a symposium of international music educators who were interested in philosophy. Ideas that challenged Reimer's philosophical stance—music education as aesthetic education—were debated and brought to the attention of the music education profession.

David Elliott (1995) presented his philosophical ideas for music education in the monograph *Music Matters: A New Philosophy of Music Education*. Elliott espouses the praxial philosophical stance. Praxialists contend that there are no artistic universals for meaning in music, that music has a variety of meanings per culture, and that music is an "action (overt *and* covert) that is purposeful, contextual, and critically reflective . . . " (Elliott, 1996–7, p. 22). Music performance is the primary tool for learning music, and it is through performance that musical intelligence is developed.

Music as a Core Subject

During the 1980s, there was a renewed interest in giving attention to the "basic" subjects in public school curricula. In addition, teachers were being held "accountable" for meeting basic schoolwide, state, and national curricula criteria in core subject areas. During his term as president of the United States, George Herbert Walker Bush proposed legislation that focused on the rejuvenation of education in "core" academic domains. The arts, however, were not included in this proposal. Therefore, representatives from dance, theater, visual arts, and music lobbied for the inclusion of the arts as a core subject. The creation of voluntary national music standards came, in part, as a response to President Bill Clinton's approval of *Goals 2000: Educate America Act*, in which arts as an integral part of the school music experience were placed into federal law.

In 1994, MENC, as a partner of the Consortium of National Arts Education Associations, published the *National Standards for Arts Education* (dance, music, theater, and visual arts). The document examines philosophical questions such as, "What is art?," "Who are the artists?," "Who benefits from arts education?," and "Are arts important to life and learning?" Other considerations are multiculturalism, diversity, technology, assessment, meaningful artistic experience, curricular integration, and competencies in each artistic domain for students in each grade level.

Music Makes Students Smarter

Learning music and participating in musical experiences is typically accompanied by some degree of personal enjoyment and self-fulfillment. In recent years, however, the media, *basing their messages on loose research findings*, have spread the news that music makes children smarter. The question of how music is processed in the brains of young children has intrigued researchers, especially because of the latest technological tools that assist the researchers in their investigations (Flohr, Miller, and Persellin, 1996; Rauscher, Shaw, and Ky, 1993).

Frances Rauscher said that she and her colleagues "have found short-term improvement of college students' performance of spatial-temporal tasks after the students listened to a Mozart sonata" (Costa-Giomi et al., 1999, p. 31). This phenomenon became known as the "Mozart Effect." In addition, Rauscher's research of preschool children's brain activity during music listening suggested that "children who had received music instruction scored higher in spatial task ability than those who had not" (Flohr, Miller, and Persellin, 1999). Immediately the media, and many public school music educators, jumped on the Mozart bandwagon as a means of justifying music education in the schools. If students could score better on standardized tests as a result of receiving music education, then all students would benefit from music education—an extramusical reason for valuing music education in the schools.

Results of the "brain and music" research, however, have caused much debate (Demorest and Morrison, 2000; Flohr, Miller, and Persellin, 1996; Reimer, 1999). Though their reports have caused quite an enthusiastic stir in the music education community, some of the findings were based on research that tested the short-term effects of musical exposure. Consequent studies attempting to replicate the Rauscher and Shaw studies seem not to indicate similar findings.

While music educators have long believed that music experiences at an early age influence children's brain development, there are many other variables that contribute to the developmental process that may or may not have to do with early musical experiences. With additional technological advances, researchers might provide concrete evidence of the specific effects musical experience has on brain activity and development.

Music Education for the Future

As the new millennium approached, MENC President June Hinckley led the effort to reassess and redefine music education as a profession, along with the values and expectations that are held at the core of the profession's existence. This effort resulted in *Vision 2020: The Housewright Symposium on the Future of Music Education*, held in 1999, at Florida State University, Tallahassee, Florida. The Housewright Symposium included music educators from all areas within the music education profession. Questions considered at the symposium (Madsen, 2000) are shaping the current music education profession.

- Why do humans value music?
- Why study music?
- How can skills and current knowledge be taught through the music content standards?

- How can all people continue to be involved in meaningful musical participation?
- How will societal and technological changes affect the teaching of music?
- What should be the relationship between schools and other sources of learning?

Notice that while the times have changed, the questions have not. The Housewright Declaration, the result of the symposium, holds the following principles (Madsen, 2000, p. 219). Teaching, learning, and assessment strategies affected by these principles also were presented in the complete document, *Vision 2020* (Madsen, 2000).

> "Music clearly must have important value for people."
> "Music makes a difference in people's lives."
> "Music is a basic way of knowing and doing because of its own nature and because of the relationship of that nature to the human condition . . ."
> "Societal and technological changes will have an enormous impact for the future of music education."
> "Music educators must . . . ensure that the best of the Western art tradition and other musical traditions are transmitted to future generations."

MENC's latest statement of music education philosophy is the result of years of discussion and debate over the questions that you, as a pre-service music educator, are also considering. The statement is a part of the MENC *Membership Handbook* (2000).

> Through its many programs, activities, publications, and conferences, MENC addresses all aspects of music education and works to ensure that every student shall have access and exposure to a balanced, comprehensive and high quality program of music instruction.
> Toward the end of promoting the best possible music education for all children and advancing music education as a profession, MENC's objectives are to:

- Provide information, resources, and services for music education professionals
- Provide a forum for the exchange of ideas through publications and meetings
- Promote music as an essential area of study
- Foster the utilization of the most effective techniques and resources in music education
- Investigate curriculum needs and develop resources for effective music education
- Develop criteria, guidelines, and evaluation procedures for music education

- Encourage excellence in music education by recognizing individual achievements and contributions to the profession
- Maintain an effective liaison with national organizations that have allied interests in arts and music education."

Your Philosophy Statement

Pondering the myriad questions and the insurmountable information in this chapter and from your own educational experiences can be quite overwhelming, a bit confusing at the very least. Did your perception of music education change as a result of reading the ideas of prominent thinkers? Were you able to make the connection between the evolution of music education in the schools and world events? Did you resonate with any of the philosophical perspectives presented in this chapter? Were you skeptical of any of the philosophical ideas?

While you might not (and probably will not!) have a solid philosophy of music education, you are most likely at the point of being able to take inventory of some of your values at this point of your music education journey. Return to the who, what, when, where, why, and how questions from the beginning of the chapter. Think about which of your values are musical or extramusical. Use the chart on the following page to organize your thoughts and then attempt to write a brief statement of your music education values and passions. Good luck!

At the end of four or five years, many of you will graduate with a degree in music education. You will begin the process of looking for a job. One of the questions that most school administrators ask of an interviewee is, "What is your personal philosophy of music education?"—what do you value and why. You, too, might raise the same issues with the interviewers: What is the school district's perspective of music education? What are its expectations for a music education program within the school district? A good match between prospective employee and school district is partially dependent on philosophical stances that are basically in agreement.

Final (Beginning?) Thoughts

The authors' intent in writing this text has been to provide the reader with an introduction to the music education profession: tools, methodologies, students, historical accounts, challenges, and philosophies. But as the text's title, *Prelude to Music Education*, suggests, the curtain has been raised, but the main theatrical drama—teaching, learning, reflecting—has just begun to unfold. Your initial exploration marks the beginning of your professional

Values Inventory

	Musical	*Extramusical*
Who?		
What?		
Where?		
When?		
Why?		
How?		

journey. As a result of reading this text, completing the assignments, and discussing questions pertinent to the music education profession, has your interest in the music education profession changed? If so, how? Has reading about a specific area of music education sparked an interest that you will choose to pursue? How might you pursue your interests in music education? What role do you want to play in providing students with music instruction? What are your professional dreams for the future of music education?

Remember . . . YOU are the future of music education. YOU can make a substantial difference in the lives of children that you teach. YOU are on an important journey. May your professional journey be as rewarding, satisfying, surprising, and joyful as the journeys that the authors have taken individually and together as colleagues.

As good teachers weave the fabric that joins them with students and subjects, the heart is the loom on which the threads are tied, the tension held, the shuttle flies, and the fabric is stretched tight. Small wonder, then, that teaching tugs at the heart, opens the heart, even breaks the heart. . . . The courage to teach is the courage to keep one's heart open in those very moments when the heart is asked to hold more than it is able so that the teacher and students and subject can be woven into the fabric of community that learning and living require. (Palmer, 1998, p. 11)

QUESTIONS FOR DISCUSSION

(You might choose to use the questions posed in this section and throughout this chapter as means for organizing and formulating your own philosophy of music education statement.)

- What do you consider the current public perception of music education to be? Why?
- What reforms in music education would you like to implement? Provide a rationale for each reform that you suggest.
- How might the *National Standards for Arts Education* influence music education reform? Cite specific examples.
- What does a music teacher do to establish an image within a school or community setting?
- What image do you want to project as a music educator?
- What image do you want your music program to project to others (i.e., what is most important to you in your music program)?
- How do the following aspects of music education interact: Image, values, philosophy, curriculum?

ASSIGNMENTS

I. Developing your philosophy of music education
   A. Present a statement of your present philosophy of music education. Be sure to include something of the role of music in society and or the importance of music to human life, the function of the school with respect to those roles/values, and what the nature of music instruction should be—by whom, of what (content, performance and/or nonperformance classes, to whom, and so on).
   B. Be certain that for every statement in your philosophy, you provide justification. Empty comments without supporting rationale and evidence make for a weak philosophical statement. Your philosophy of music education

should reflect your thinking as a teacher and your experience providing music instruction. It should not represent the perspective of a student ("In my high school experience . . . , when I was in high school . . . , and so on).

C. After you write your philosophy of music education, discuss the following questions:

1. Which questions provided the most challenge in the preparation of your statement of philosophy?

2. Have there been any changes in your ideas about music, or music's role in society during the current semester?

3. To what extent are schools with which you are familiar able to implement your philosophy of music education? What does/would such implementation require of teachers? of administrators? of the community?

II. Defending your program

A. Divide your class into small groups. Each group should address one of the following issues by providing rationales for the existence of the music programs. After a group has presented its position on the issue, students who are not in that group are encouraged to "play devil's advocate" so that a debate might ensue.

B. Choose from the following issues (one per group):

1. You teach at a middle school where students have to choose between chorus, orchestra, band. They meet at the same time of the day. Also, a student in a performance ensemble does not need to take general music. What is you defense for having general music for all students, regardless of performance? What is your recommendation about the schedule conflicts?

2. There is no string program in your school district. Why do you want to initiate one?

3. The marching band is fully funded. You want to start a concert band. What would be your rationale?

4. Justify the existence of general music/nonperformance classes as a part of a balanced secondary school program.

5. Your school has a "no religious music" policy. What are your thoughts concerning a balanced choral program?

6. Your principal does not understand why you have sectional rehearsals as a part of your schedule. What is your rationale?

7. Your school board intends to eliminate music for kindergartners as taught by the music specialist. What is your response and course of action?

III. Teaching scenarios

The following paragraphs describe a general music education class. Each scenario reflects a teacher's specific values, some of the values being different for each scenario. As you read the scenarios, determine the teacher's values, and how they are reflected in the musical experiences provided for the students in the general music classroom. Provide reasons for your choices.

A. After listening to "Spiritual" as sung by Sweet Honey in the Rock, the middle school students will analyze its formal properties, which include phrasing and the use of choral refrain. In addition, the students will discuss melodic shape (direction) within each of the phrases, metric flow, and the use of dynamics.

B. After listening to "Spiritual" as sung by Sweet Honey in the Rock, the middle school students will analyze the formal properties, including phrasing and the use of choral refrain. In addition, the students will discuss melodic shape (direction) within each of the phrases. At the conclusion of the lesson, the students will discuss their own affective response to the music as well as contextual information (social-cultural-historical information).

C. After listening to "Spiritual" as sung by Sweet Honey in the Rock, the middle school students will describe images that are formulated in the mind as they listened to the music. They will also describe specific emotions that are attached to that piece, as related to the intent of the performer and composer. An important part of the song's analysis will be the relaying of the "story" that accompanies the musical properties and how the listeners (the students) can relate to the story (as told through the lyrics).

D. In order to learn about spirituals, students will learn to sing a spiritual entitled, "Nobody Knows the Trouble I've Seen." Students will also learn to sing a song that incorporates solo-response form. Following this activity, students will be asked to respond to the teacher's "call" on classroom melody and rhythm instruments. The responses are learned melodic and rhythmic patterns that the children learned in the class last week.

REFERENCES

Books and Articles

ABELES, H., HOFFER, C., and KLOTMAN, R. (1994). *Foundations of Music Education* (second ed.). New York: Schirmer.

COSTA-GIOMI, E., PRICE, H., RAUSCHER, F., SCHMIDT, J., SHACKFORD, M., and SIMS, W. (1999, December). "Straight Talk about Music and Brain Research." *Teaching Music*, 7(3), pp. 29–35.

DAY, S. (1640). *Bay Psalm Book*. Cambridge, MA: np.

DEMOREST, S. and MORRISON, S. (2000, September). "Does Music Make You Smarter?" *Music Educators Journal*, 87(2), pp. 33–9.

ELLIOTT, D. (1995). *Music Matters: A New Philosophy of Music Education*. New York: Oxford University Press.

ELLIOTT, D. (1996–7). "Putting Matters in Perspective: Reflections on a New Philosophy." *The Quarterly Journal of Music Teaching and Learning*, 7(2–4), pp. 20–35.

FLOHR, J., MILLER, D., and PERSELLIN, D. (1996). *Children's Electrophysical Responses to Music*. Paper presented at the 22nd International Society of Music Education World Conference, Amsterdam, The Netherlands (ERIC Document PS025654).

FLOHR, J., MILLER, D., and PERSELLIN, D. (1999, June). "Recent Brain Research on Young Children." *Teaching Music*, 6(6), pp. 41–3, 54.

JORGENSEN, E. (1997). *In Search of Music Education*. Urbana: University of Illinois Press.

MADSEN, C. (ed.). (2000). *Vision 2020: The Housewright Symposium on the Future of Music Education*. Reston, VA: MENC.

MARK, M. (1986). *Contemporary Music Education* (second ed.). New York: Schirmer.

MARK, M. (2000). "MENC: From Tanglewood to the Present." In Madsen, C. (ed.), *Vision 2020: The Housewright Symposium on the Future of Music Education*. Reston, VA: MENC.

MUSIC EDUCATORS NATIONAL CONFERENCE (MENC). (1994). *National Standards for Arts Education*. Reston, VA: MENC.

MUSIC EDUCATORS NATIONAL CONFERENCE (MENC). (2000). *Membership Handbook*. Reston, VA: MENC.

PALMER, P. (1998). *The Courage to Teach: Exploring the Inner Landscape of a Teacher's Life*. San Francisco: Jossey-Bass Publishers.

RAUSCHER, F., SHAW, G., and KY, K. (1993). "Music and Spatial Task Performance." *Nature*, 365, p. 611.

REIMER, B. (1989). *A Philosophy of Music Education*. Englewood Cliffs, NJ: Prentice Hall.

REIMER, B. (1999, July). "Facing the Risks of the 'Mozart Effect.'" *Music Educators Journal*, 86(1), pp. 37–43.

Valuable Resources

REED, R. and JOHNSON, T. (1996). *Philosophical Documents in Education*. New York: Longman Press.

International Journal of Education and Art. <http://ijea.asu.edu/index.html>

Appendix

TENTATIVE COURSE CALENDAR

#	Date	Content	Assignment Due
1	9/04	Course Overview—Introduction of Music Education Faculty	
2	9/06	*"My Most Influential Teacher"*	Chapter 1 two-minute student presentations **Bring videotape!**
3	9/11		Chapter 2, journals begin
4	9/13	Lesson Planning	
5	9/18	Interviewing	Lesson plan due
6	9/20	Verbal/Nonverbal delivery	
7	9/25	Report on interviews	Interview due
8	9/27	Advising Info—Professional Development—MEAO	
9	10/02	Music Ed Technology—description sheet, demonstrations	Chapter 11
10	10/04	"How To" presentations	Student present, Videotape
11	10/09	"How To" presentations	Student present, Videotape
12	10/11	Discuss observations (two by this time)	
13	10/16	Classroom Management	Journals due
	10/20	Autumn Recess	
	10/22	Autumn Recess	
14	10/27	Current approaches:—pre-K–5, General Music	Chapters 3, 4
15	10/29	Current approaches: String Education	Chapter 7
16	11/03	Current approaches: Band Performances	Chapter 6
17	11/05	Current approaches: Secondary general/choral	Chapters 5, 8
18	11/10	Dalcroze Eurhythmics	
19	11/12	Presentations	Student presentations on research (topic of their choice) bring in bibliography (*two sources*)

20	11/17	Presentations	
21	11/19	Career Options	
22	11/24	*Day off (no class)* attend presentations in lieu of class today	Attend one of four principal's "Issues" class discussions
23	12/01	Special Learners	Chapter 10
24	12/03	Multicultural Music Education	Chapter 9
25	12/08	Lifelong learning	Journals due
26	12/10	Philosophy	Chapter 12, Philosophy paper due during finals

INDEX